Creative Design
in Wall Hangings

Also by the Author

THE ART AND CRAFT OF HAND WEAVING

RECTANGLES by Lili Blumenau.
Photo by Spencer Depas.

Creative Design in Wall Hangings

Weaving Patterns Based on Primitive and Medieval Art

Lili Blumenau

Crown Publishers, Inc.   New York

© 1967, by Lili Blumenau
Library of Congress Catalog Card Number: 66-26169
Printed in the United States of America
Second Printing, July, 1970

Acknowledgments

This book owes its creation to the inspiration and encouragement of many people. To name them all would require another volume in itself. Wherever possible, contributors are credited where their work appears.

My greatest thanks go to many artists of the United States, as well as to those of foreign countries, who demonstrated their art and techniques before the camera with the hope, both theirs and mine, that you would see their original work. Collectors, museums, and students were extremely generous in permitting their works to be reproduced.

I add a specific note of thanks to all the photographers whose photographs of wall hangings and procedures are used. My special thanks to Frank Long who helped me to surmount my language barrier, and René Jacques for the original technical drawings.

LILI BLUMENAU

Contents

List of Color Plates

Part 1
Wall Hangings
Past and Present

Roundel from a linen tunic, tapestry in linen and wool, between 4th and 5th centuries. *The Cooper Union Museum.*

Chapter 1
The Coptic Weavers of Egypt

A T THE DAWN OF THE CHRISTIAN ERA, EGYPTIAN CIVILIZATION HAD ceased to be a great and flourishing cradle of the arts and was in the throes of cultural chaos. Its influence had begun to wane even earlier, but by the first century A.D. Mediterranean handicraftsmen no longer turned to Egypt for creative inspiration. Its art-producing activities had come to an almost complete standstill, in the sense that nothing original and new was being produced; and the old, widely copied decorative motifs—always so formalized that they could hardly be said to be strikingly original—were being repeated in so lackluster a way that their artistry had completely vanished.

In the fifth century, however, under the influence of the Coptic Church, Egypt developed a new kind of creative expression, and regained her former artistic supremacy. It was during this century, and until the Mohammedan Conquest, that the Copts—those descendants of the ancient Egyptians who professed a modified form of Christianity—painted elaborate murals, built domed basilicas, made limestone carvings, and wove textiles in linen and wool that were remarkably intricate and beautiful.

Coptic tapestries from the fifth century on are of unusual interest to the present-day weaver not only because the designs showed a fully developed style and were unique in their expressiveness but also because they depicted a way of life that existed contemporary with, but quite apart from, the decaying Roman Empire. Roman motifs in general were of a quite different nature, particularly in the related field of ornamental pottery making, even though the invading Roman legions forced the Coptic weavers to bow occasionally to Roman taste. What adds to the appeal of these tapestries is the fact that, unlike Byzantine art, which also existed independently of Rome, Coptic art seems to us today to be vibrantly alive and the opposite of stylized.

By studying these rich and colorful fabrics we can gain a startlingly accurate idea of how fifth-century Egyptians conducted their daily lives— how they dressed, dined, participated in ritual ceremonies, engaged in trade, and prepared the dead for burial. The ancient Egyptian custom of

3

embalming, for instance, was still practiced; but instead of wrapping the corpse in linen bands and preserving it without burial, they dressed the embalmed remains in garments worn during life, and burial took place immediately. Lifelike portraits of the dead, painted on canvas, were either wrapped around the bodies or placed over the faces of the deceased.

Egyptian treasures from the past were unearthed by archaeologists as far back as the beginning of the nineteenth century, and the splendor of not a few of these antiquities so excited Europeans that better-equipped expeditions were later organized and the Coptic tapestries rescued from oblivion. They can now be studied in museums all over the world.

In the fifth and sixth centuries the Copts dressed quite simply. Rich and poor alike wore undyed tunics of plain-woven linen, and these were decorated with bright tapestry ornaments. They were one-piece garments, spread out flat at front and back to form crosses, and with a slitted aperture for the head.

Occasionally the tunics were elaborate, with very large shoulder bands terminating in a pendant decoration. The motifs in the fully developed Coptic style of the fifth to eighth centuries were largely symbolic; and when they were not woven crosses in quite beautiful mosaic effect, they depicted scenes from the Bible—the Adoration of the Magi, the story of David, or the miracle at Cana.

The development of Coptic weaving can be traced in the variations of design on the wearing apparel of fifth-to-eighth-century Egyptians. Not only do the invented decorations alone display a continuously evolving, if not always more intricate, decorative style—they also show how Christian symbols were used more and more frequently as the new religion replaced the paganism of earlier centuries among a constantly increasing number of worshipers.

There are two different styles in the tapestries found in Coptic cemeteries—the invented and the naturalistic. The naturalistic designs were predominately pagan in motif—with fauns and satyrs and men and women locked in combat with animals, and there can be no doubt at all that these scenes were suggested by the entertainments of the Roman amphitheater. By the fifth century the developed Coptic style had become almost entirely Christian in inspiration, and was no longer naturalistic or Greco-Roman. Christian themes predominated; and when they were not symbolic of Christianity, vines and flowering plants alternated with intricately woven decorative scrolls.

Seemingly there were a few pagan survivals as late as the eighth century, but Christian emblems were by then used almost exclusively.

Coptic tapestries made use of powerful color effects, and many of the designs were so boldly original and contrasting that they must have dazzled the eye of the beholder. Sometimes they verged on the grotesque.

Curiously enough, however, the weave constructions used by the Copts were few in number. They had the ability to achieve impressive aesthetic effects without employing a wide variety of warp-and-weft variations. The purely functional need for closely woven fabrics to protect them from the elements may have been an influencing factor in keeping weave variations at a minimum, since loosely woven garments would have been poor substitutes for the ones they habitually wore throughout the year. So great was their need, indeed, for more warmth and protection in their winter garments that they invented a loop-pile technique in which long and short loops of wool were drawn out of the weft.

Egypt is famous throughout the world today for its cotton, but in ancient times fine linen was the fabric most prized by the ruling caste. The wives or the Pharaohs wore linen garments, and ancient Egyptian textiles were made of linen warp and weft. In the fifth to eighth centuries Coptic tapestries were of linen warp and wool weft. There are many designs in early Coptic pieces in which this combination was employed for weaving embroidery effects.

In Egypto-Coptic graves there have been found a few fragments of silk fabrics, in the form of decorative squares and roundels. We cannot be certain as to the origin of this silk, but it probably found its way to Egypt through the enterprise of two Persian monks of the sixth century. These monks were employed by the Emperor Justinian, and were said to have been the first to introduce Chinese silkworms into the East. The silk culture of Persia and Egypt can perhaps be traced back to this instance of legendary smuggling. We know, in any case, that the Coptic weavers managed to obtain a certain amount of silk.

Archaeologists have failed to unearth a single Coptic loom or spinning device, but there can be little doubt that Egyptian looms were primitive types of upright and low-warp looms. The normally vertical warp threads in Coptic textiles were so irregular that weights must have been used for the tension of the warp. The irregularity may have been deliberate, however, and prompted solely by aesthetic considerations.

In the Coptic cemeteries near Sakkara, Ahurim, and Antonoe, wooden combs and spindles have been found—all that remains of the tools on which the Egyptian handweavers wrought their miracles of design.

Tunics were usually woven in a combination of plain weave and tapestry. The number of warp threads remained the same all the way through, but a division took place wherever an ornament was used.

The burial portrait fabrics that covered the faces of the dead were often in the geometric style of an earlier period—a style that can be traced back to the fashionable garments of undyed linen and purple wool that were worn in the third and fourth centuries.

One can only speculate as to just how often the Coptic weavers started off with preconceived ideas and did not depart from them until the finished tapestry was removed from the loom. That they occasionally shunned experimentation we know, for a few of the designs have a one-track kind of consistency that could have been produced in no other way. But in general the tapestries are the opposite of rigid in design; and that the Copts possessed fertile imaginations, and were more experimental than otherwise, seems incontrovertible. If they were ever at a loss for motifs, the tapestries that have survived across the centuries provide very little evidence that such an occurrence took place frequently or caused them serious concern.

It can be said with confidence that they had a superlative feeling for both materials and form. They did not neglect one at the expense of the other, and their color sense seems to have been so highly developed that only a very few of the great medieval tapestries surpass the Coptic color combinations in strength and brilliance. Many of the colors were bold indeed, even clashed on occasion. But colors that never clash seem at times to suggest a certain poverty of imagination and a lack of aesthetic perceptiveness and daring.

In all their tapestries the Coptic weavers paid meticulous attention to detail. In the naturalistic tapestries the mantle of reality was intricately constructed; in the symbolic ones there was a soaring kind of fantasy that seems at times completely modern.

The individuality of the Coptic weaving has a great deal to teach the contemporary weaver-craftsman. Not only do they furnish inspiration in our time. Many of the innovations that the Egyptian tapestry makers introduced almost two millenniums ago are thoroughly applicable to modern design.

Polychrome tapestries in linen and wool, Egypt, between 4th and 5th centuries. *The Cooper Union Museum.*

Tapestry with pomegranate branches, 5th century. *The Cooper Union Museum.*

Classical figures in fine tapesty weave, Egypt, 5th century. *The Cooper Union Museum.*

Coptic roundel, part of a tunic. The tapestry represents The
Adoration of the Magi. Between 7th and 8th centuries. *The
Cooper Union Museum.*

Chapter 2
The Pre-Incan and Incan Tapestries of Peru

B Y THE YEAR 1200—THREE CENTURIES BEFORE THE DISCOVERY OF America—Peruvian civilization had reached a degree of perfection comparable to the high periods of Egyptian culture, which it somewhat resembles. The dead were wrapped in layers of beautiful cloth, and utensils, created and used during life, were put into the graves.

These vessels were often decorated with representations of human, animal, and geometric figures. Some were painted with figures in costume and were shown wearing elaborate headdresses. On other vessels there were decorations portraying weavers and looms. Workbaskets containing tools and yarns are also found in many of the graves. Spindles of beautiful design, covered with cotton or wool, have been found, as well as weaving sticks and swords. These artifacts, of striking design, are made of good material. And they were well preserved by the dry sand of the coastal desert cemeteries.

The dating of Peruvian artifacts and textiles is tentative. Recent excavations have produced woven materials that are believed to be at least two thousand years old. Since the Indians had no knowledge of writing, traditions were communicated by word of mouth, from one generation to the next. It was not until the Spanish conquest of Peru, in the 1530's, that Indian cultural traditions and ideas were put into writing.

Archaeologists, in their study of superimpositions and refuse during excavation, have added to our understanding of the lives of early Indians.

Magnificent old textiles have been found in graves along the southern coast of Peru. They are products of the Nascan culture, and date from the fifth century. The embroidered grave wrappings of another group, the Paracas, may be earlier. Mantles woven by the natives of the Paracas Peninsula are, in regard to decoration and size, unique in the history of weaving. On Peru's northern coast equally archaic Chimu textiles have been found, but they are less well preserved because of the wetness of the climate. However, Chimu pottery gives evidence of weaving practice during the early period.

Figures in tunics and mantles, as well as weavers at looms, are depicted on Chimu vessels. The Nasca and Chimu coastal Indians flourished for several centuries, contemporary with the development of Peruvian culture and weaving in the mountain country. Exchange of raw material between the highlands and the coastal regions resulted in the development of a middle period or style. Products of this second period (700–1200) are called Tiahuanaco—architecture, pottery, and textiles that bear a striking similarity to modern or present-day creations.

The Andean Tiahuanaco textiles exhibit great talent and culture in weaving knowledge, and were based on religious interest and feeling. In 1250–1532, when the Incas came to power, this developed Andean style continued. Textiles woven at this time were technically perfect and possessed strong feeling for color. But in this late or third period sensibility, refinement, and mysticism are less evident in the weavers' expressions.

The primitive floating loom was used by these ancient weavers, as it is today in Mexico and Guatemala. Essential parts in this loom are the two rods that hold the warp in place. The end rods have a cord secured along their length. This cord, extending from end to end of the rod, is fastened to it by another cord wound in spiral. The spiral and transverse cords are similar to a modern loom's stick-and-apron connection. Warping the two cord-wound end rods together proceeds as follows:

The warping yarn is estimated according to length and width of fabric desired. The yarn is secured around the end of one of the rods. It is alternated over and under the cord along the rod, the width of the proposed fabric, forming a warping cross, as on contemporary warping frames. The two rods are thus warped together, and the width and length of the warp, together with the end rods, make a complete loom. To each end is affixed a strong belt of tape, one to go around the weaver's waist and the other—the opposite belt—to be hitched over a hook, post, or other device. The weaver draws the loom tautly, slanting in downward toward his body as he tenses the warp.

A pair of string heddle rods is used to lift odd and even warp threads on this extremely primitive loom. The pre-Incan shuttle was thin and long. The weaver very frequently used newly spun yarn off the spindle instead of a shuttle. Intricate and subtle weaves, remarkable for their beauty, were obtained with simple instruments.

The fibers used were cotton from the Peruvian coast and mountain wool. The cotton or wool were in shades ranging from white to reddish brown. Vicuna, alpaca, and llama fibers were employed. The alpaca wool added additional attractive colors, bluish-gray, dark gray, and black. These natural colors, used in combination with vivid reds and blues in expert dyes, made striking and beautiful contrasts.

The Peruvian weavers also used other raw materials. Maguey, a hemp type of bast fiber derived from cactus stalk, had been frequently employed by the Indians in preweaving times. Peruvian fabrics were also decorated with shells and feathers. Sometimes small, disklike threaded shells were woven into the cloth, a technique that modern weavers have always favored. In the main, however, feather-woven fabrics were the height of style in Peruvian taste.

Weave variations were abundant, ranging from plain weave and brocade to the most intricate gauze. Peruvian tapestry is even more complex than Flemish and French. Twill and rib variations were common, as well as masterly designs in double and triple cloth. The techniques are an endless inspiration. There is much feeling for material and composition, particularly for embroidered cloth. The Paracas fabric structure of varied stitches in relation to open plain weave is an excellent example of how effective this kind of variation can be. The fringes and tassels are tied in the most elegant way in many of these fabrics, and there are also fabrics with versatile knitted borders.

Further, the Peruvians invented a very unusual kind of pile weave. Ordinary pile weave consists of warp and weft with rows of knots alternating with picks in plain weave; or the pile is effected with a second warp. But the Peruvians created a mesh ground especially well suited to holding knots.

In their use of ornament and color treatment, the pre-Incan weavers have much to teach us about designing, even though we do not use yarn and color to interpret figures as they did. Today the weaver gains more by studying the highly expressive skills and techniques displayed in Peruvian textiles than he does by mechanically copying or by trying to reproduce the elusive charm of their motifs—demon gods, rows of llamas ascending a mountain trail, and the like. Art in weaving depends on how one transforms a pattern, whether it is a twill weave or a fish motif.

Ornament in the early Tiahuanaco period was singularly devoid of naturalism. Symbolic motifs were arranged in intricate and stylized patterns. Even human heads were transformed into geometrics, and these motifs were distributed in various sizes and directions.

Backgrounds are not infrequently divided into large and small bands. The narrow strips have no decoration, but the principal ones are divided into rectangles. Abstract motifs symbolizing the human figure, in all-over patterns, are contained in these squares.

The power of Tiahuanaco and other Indian textiles resides not only in the Peruvian talent for inventing unusual shapes and arrangements but also in the deft use of values. Variations of light and dark are often drastic, but through volume and skillful placement of color and design unity is created. Red, blue, and yellow appear in various intensities, in combination with neutrals. Typical color schemes consist of three reds and four neutrals. In many of these combinations the hues are pink, bright rose, and purplish-red, with light tan, ocher yellow, light and dark brown.

On late Chimu textiles bird and fish motifs are severely formalized in geometrics. A tan and brown double cloth design consists of large-size zigzags with the bands forming birds, often of fantastic plumage, and the points consisting of a fish motif.

Here there is no difference between background and motif—both are treated with emphasis. Another early Chimu example is bordered with large birds, their tails meandering in Greek key design. They are brocaded in light-tan or dark-brown plain weave.

The pre-Incas, like professional weavers and their customers today, had considerable taste for sheer material. In a blue crepe cloth with vertical and horizontal stripes we can admire a warp and weft arrangement similar to some of ours.

The stripe and plaid patterns in the Peruvian work are neither stripes nor plaids. The secret of this rather mysterious transformation—the designs merely approximate plaids—may lie in the varying amount of threads in varying open and closed spaces. However the effect is produced, it is certainly an unusual one.

It is profitable to study examples of early Peruvian weaving at close hand and most attentively in museums. New and unsuspected beauties will be revealed if we return to them again and again, as never-failing sources of inspiration. In their bold and unusual contrasts—dark and light backgrounds are used in a wholly individual way, to provide an imaginatively exciting kind of depth imagery—their highly original color combinations and weft-and-warp variations, there is no other source material so closely related to contemporary creative weaving. Whether the fabric is a doll's shirt or a tapestry with ritual significance, depicting plume-wearing warriors with the heads of condors and birds of brilliant plumage with heads that are symbolically half human, they have for the modern weaver an appeal that is irresistible and can help him solve problems in contemporary design and method as well.

Modern education has begun to encourage a wide and close acquaintance with the arts and handicrafts of the civilizations of the past, and this progressive tendency has revived, for the student of today, the vanished splendor of the early Peruvian cultures. We know now that the Old World was not alone in creating objects of imperishable beauty and that the Incas and pre-Incas were as accomplished as the Egyptians in their mastery of structural design in the service of beauty.

Figure of a Peruvian, embroidered in the Paracas style, pre-Inca, 2nd to 6th centuries. *The Metropolitan Museum of Art.*

Tapestry fragment, about A.D. 800, Tiahuanaco period. *The Cooper Union Museum.*

Fragment of dark-brown cotton cloth with fishes, from the pre-Inca period, late Chimu culture, 14th century. *The Metropolitan Museum of Art.*

Opposite, top left:
Transparent fragment with tapestry border, pre-Colombian. *Collection, Lili Blumenau.*

Opposite, top right:
Tapestry fragment, geometrical motifs, between 14th and 15th centuries. *Collection, Lili Blumenau.*

Opposite, bottom:
Cotton gauze from Peru, between 12th and 13th centuries. *The Cooper Union Museum.*

17

Chapter 3
The Medieval Weavers

ANY FIGURED TEXTILES WERE WOVEN IN THE PAST ALL OVER the world. They speak for their times, for other places, other civilizations. For instance, European weaving was based on Egyptian cultures combined with the influence of Persian design of the time of the Sassanids who ruled around 600 to 700 C.E. These Persian designers are believed to have learned their intricate patterns from the Chinese. Still later influences were Byzantine, which itself was influenced by Saracenic, or Arabic, weaving.

Sassanid and Byzantine design, which is formal, but manages to represent or suggest objects, was especially popular. The underlying plan in Oriental textiles consisted of circular bands forming a roundel. These roundels with motifs within and around were repeated at more or less regular intervals. The spaces within and around the circles are decorated with animals, fantastic and real, some facing each other, some placed back to back. In the thirteenth or fourteenth century the circular framework was elongated, approaching more or less a large shape like the letter *o* in writing. Such a framework or composition plan was characteristic for Gothic areas.

Naturally, only small parts of medieval silks are preserved, and may be seen in various museums all over the world. Some of these fragments that are styled or composed in this formal way are from Syria or Byzantium, between the eighth and tenth centuries. One example shows predominantly one large roundel and only small parts of the other circles. The large visible roundel contains a stylized figure in the center surrounded by two lions. It is called The Lion Strangler, a symbolic subject frequently used in the Middle Ages. Between these large and small circles are stylized foliages, that is, leaves and flowers not realistically expressed.

Another fragment, made between the eighth and ninth centuries, also Byzantine, has a different, more simplified, geometrical composition. For instance, here the framework around smaller circles consists of stars with four points. Within these stars are stripes, horizontal and vertical, dark and light, in irregular dimensions. The entire background for the small roundels is dark. Inside one of these circles is a bird, recognizable but simplified according to style. The bird circles alternate with a row of others, of which each contains a tree. The ornaments or patterns mentioned on the fragments resemble the Egyptian Coptic tapestries. The principal difference here is the representation of the weaving skill, as well as the fact that the subjects or motifs are repeated in the same fashion on the entire width of the fabric.

The very large medieval tapestries form another division. They were naturally much stiffer textiles than the pliable medieval silks. These wall-size hangings or tapestries were woven in France as early as A.D. 711. One of the principle centers or ateliers was in Aubusson. It was here that the group called "Apocalypse" was woven. It was commissioned in Angers in 1377 by the Duc d'Anjou from Nicolas Bataille. In 1937, 560 years later, these tapestries still exerted a profound influence on most of the creations produced in the ateliers of Aubusson.

Another important influence in the development of tapestry weaving was a work by the great artist and tapestry designer Raphael. In 1514 he executed a series called "The Acts of the Apostles." The production was done in Brussels. The result was so successful that for the next 150 years Brussels manufactured one set after another of the Raphael innovations. In 1662, Jean-Baptiste Colbert, French adviser to Louis XIV, called upon his country's makers of tapestries to create new designs and innovations to please the king, as well as to contribute to the prosperity of France. In the king's name he took over the Manufactory of the Gobelins, which is still one of the most famous factories in Paris. He also supervised to some extent the tapestry ateliers in Beauvais. The best painters of the day and about eight hundred weavers worked for these studios. Now the painter had to learn to paint with yarns.

Science also contributed to the expansion of the tapestry industry. Around 1839 a chemist named Michel Eugène Chevreul headed the Gobelins factory. He devised a palette of 10 circles of clear colors. Each was divided into 72 scales, each with 20 tones, for the enormous total of 14,400 tones. But even that was not enough. By assembling two threads of different tones to create a third, he raised the total possible number of combinations to nearly 200 million.

During the first part of the twentieth century the reputation of the Aubusson weavers declined. By then the weavers worked on old-fashioned clichés—on cartoons pieced together from fragments. They repainted worn-out parts, and changed the design if they felt inclined. Because the products were inferior and the prices astronomical, they soon lost their profitable market. Between 1928 and 1930 half of the remaining workshops in Aubusson closed, and three-fourths of the weavers gave up their craft.

In 1939 the head of Gobelins Beauvais telegraphed to the famous painter and tapestry weaver Jean Lurçat to meet him in Aubusson. There was an urgency to his appeal. In a desperate effort to keep Aubusson weaving alive, the Ministry of National Education commissioned Lurçat to work with the atelier owners and weavers to produce four works entitled "The Four Seasons." The painters Marcel Gromaire and Pierre Dubreuil were given identical commissions.

By 1943, Jean Lurçat and other french tapestry artists were holding shows in Toulouse. In March, 1944, they displayed twenty works in occupied Paris. From then on, the weaving creations of the French artists began to regain their stature. Well versed in weaving technique and materials, these artists were capable of weaving their own designs. But for practical purposes, they don't. It takes too much time, and the weaving is better left in the hands of master craftsmen, who do nothing else. The artist's design or cartoon is done in full scale on heavy paper. Some artists, for instance Jean Lurçat, do their designs in black-and-white outline. Each area is given a number corresponding to the number assigned to a color of yarn that has been given by the artists to the weaver. The rest of the artists do their cartoons in full color, with yarn swatches also provided to show what the exact color of the wool must be.

In the first years of redisciplining Aubusson weavers, the artists were rigorous in their prescription. Weavers were not allowed to interpret. Virtually every single point was prescribed. This is still true, and members of the Association of Tapestry Painter-Designers do not allow their weavers to modify the artist's design in any way.

On the Aubusson looms the cotton warp is strung horizontally between two roller beams. The full-scale cartoon is placed face up immediately below the warp. Each unit of the pattern or background is handwoven with a weft of the required color, which is inserted back and forth only over the section where the color appears in the pattern. The weaver works from the back of the tapestry so that he can secure yarns when necessary. Thus the face of the tapestry faces the design and is a mirror image of the design. As the tapestry is produced, it is rolled up on the beam nearest the weaver.

One can see why design, as well as weaving, requires great skill. First the artist must make his design the mirror image of what he wants the tapestry to look like. Second, the weaver can never really see the face of the tapestry until it is entirely finished and off the loom. He can see a few inches of the face by putting a mirror below the warp threads.

The weavers at the beginning spend three years in school. Then they continue and work under the supervision of master weavers, some of whom have been at it forty years or more. Through their fingers fly, with great precision, the changing of bobbins with yarns. The average production of one square yard per weaver is one month. Some designs take more time.

In Gobelins the same general weaving process is used. But the warp beams are vertical. The cartoons cannot be placed immediately near the warp. Instead they are placed behind the weaver, who can turn around and look at them. An intermediate step of tracing the design direct on the warp is required. Here execution is slower. Gobelins production averages three months per square yard per weaver.

Thus the heritage of the medieval weavers, once destined for extinction, has today been revived and is once again a part of the cultural contributions of France.

THE HUNT OF THE UNICORN, French or Flemish, 15th century, wool and silk with metal threads, from the Château of Verteuil. *The Metropolitan Museum of Art, The Cloisters Collection, gift of John D. Rockefeller, Jr., 1938.*

THE HUNT OF THE UNICORN, fragment, "The Capture," French or Flemish, 15th century, wool and silk with metal threads, from the Château of Verteuil. *The Metropolitan Museum of Art, The Cloisters Collection, gift of John D. Rockefeller, Jr., 1938.*

Opposite:
LA DAME A L'ORGUE, fragment, from the Château d'Angers. *French Cultural Services, New York.*

Opposite:
Byzantine silk, between the 8th and 9th centuries. All plant and animal forms and other motifs in early medieval times were enclosed in roundels or geometrical forms. *The Cooper Union Museum.*

Two badges of rank, worn on the tunics of members of the Chinese hierarchy of the Ming dynasty, 15th century, depicting egrets among cloud bands, and woven in brilliant colors, including vermilion, black, pale pink, white, and gold thread. The squares are badges of the first and sixth ranks. *The Cooper Union Museum.*

Opposite:
With their brilliant colors and geometrical motifs, Moorish textiles are an inspiration to contemporary weavers. *(Left)* Part of a border in silk, linen, and metal. Morocco, 19th century. *(Right)* A Hispano-Moresque silk fabric dated between the 14th and 15th centuries. *The Cooper Union Museum.*

Part of an Egyptian tapestry, perhaps of the 12th century. With this simple tapestry technique a very dramatic effect is created. *The Cooper Union Museum.*

Chapter 4
The Contemporary Weavers

Tapestries and wall hangings have today assumed an importance of such proportion that they are exhibited by museums, art galleries, and contemporary craft shows throughout the United States. Unlike many of the tapestries of old, these modern wall hangings are both designed and produced by the artist-craftsman himself. He is no longer concerned with technical perfection at the expense of personal expression. Thus, in place of the old, formal tapestry traditions, he has substituted a free and individual style. Indeed, the surfaces of some of our contemporary wall hangings might seem crude to the European weaver who is still steeped in Old World tradition.

The artist-weaver of today is free to vary his surface textures to suit the spirit of his work. He expresses himself in more sculptured and uneven ways, instead of mechanically straight lines and flat surfaces. Densities vary to conform to the composition. Yarns and other raw materials are incorporated in a free style to express a personal approach. The dynamics of the resultant wall hanging are readily realized by anyone looking at it. While every wall hanging is certainly not great art, each one is usually unique to the artist-craftsman who wove it.

Today, the artist-craftsman weaves directly on the loom. He has a vision in his mind of how the wall hanging should look when completed, and he creates and improvises as he weaves. Not many trained artists are able to work in this direct manner, but in the case of the weaver the results from this method of working are often superlative.

Artist-weavers now find the strict conventions of traditional tapestry weaving too limiting. They turn to the very sources of life for their inspirations for personal expression. Such an attitude opens up many new potentials. For example, materials themselves take on great importance. They are no longer simply things to serve a technical purpose. They now impart a sensuous joy in color and texture. In this spontaneity of expression the weaver often chooses his color scheme merely by seeing all the yarns together in a basket or on shelves as he works. Form and subject, material and color, scale and density are then synthesized in a unique manner.

Many of today's wall hangings are monumental in scale, and possess a symbolic vitality. Striking colors are used: rich purples, blues, and peacock, or paon. Thick, heavy yarns produce weighty, tangled constructions. Motifs and subjects vary considerably. There are, of course, many abstractions in various sizes of stripes and squares. There are also circles or roundels, small and large, arranged in suitable composition. Impressions from landscapes are often used, sometimes in fantastic stylized form, or at other times naturalistic or abstract. Always the artist-weaver is looking for new, expressive forms. There is virtually no subject that cannot be transformed into a composition of colored yarn.

Raw material is today perhaps the primary source of inspiration. The very fine yarns are used to create lightness and thin surface texture. Then there are the soft plied wools if one wants smooth surfaces. For highlights in a very rhythmical composition all the shiny yarns are available. Silk and the synthetics come in all sizes, from thin to thick threads. With many fascinating irregular yarns, necessary uneven effects can be achieved. Specific raw materials can be combined to suit each weaver's purposes. Like yarns, colors have individual characters. They are enhanced by the way in which they are related. A wall hanging can be done in just one color, in solid form or by using many tones of red, blue, or green.

In summary, the works of contemporary weavers of wall hangings express the personal freedom to create that characterizes our present twentieth-century living. Almost anything is valid, as long as it is the personal expression of the individual artist-craftsman.

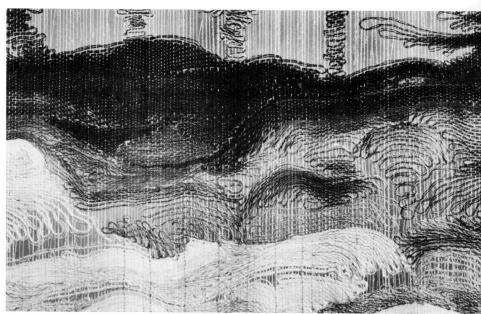

Detail of LANDSCAPE, 1958, by Lenore Tawney, U.S.A.

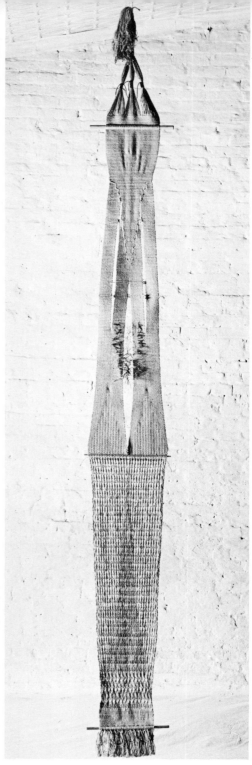

LANDSCAPE, 1958, by Lenore Tawney, U.S.A. A transparent wall hanging, 60″ x 36″, in bright-colored yarns. *Photo by Ferdinand Boesch.*

THE BRIDE, 1962, by Lenore Tawney, U.S.A. A woven form of linen with feathers, 11½′ high. *Photo by Ferdinand Boesch.*

DAYDREAM, 1965, by Mildred Fischer, U.S.A. A transparent wall hanging, 65" x 40",
in linen with strips of celanese and lace weave, in blues, greens, yellows, and white.

THE BRIDE (detail), by Lenore Tawney, U.S.A. *Photo by Ferdinand Boesch.*

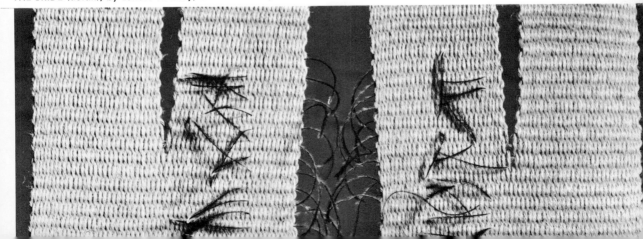

THE GIRLS IN GRAY, by Eva Autilla, Finland.
A tapestry in gray and dark-blue wool.

Tapestry, by Janice Bornt, U.S.A. Wool
and mixed fibers, 13″ x 10″.

GUARDIAN ANGEL, by Lili Blumenau, U.S.A.
A tapestry of wool and mixed fibers, in greens
and blues. *Collection Mr. & Mrs. Frederic
Breydert.*

CUSHION, by Claire Zeisler, U.S.A. A woven form, 58'' x 15'', double weave, in red and white silk, with braided ends.

CUSHION (detail), by Claire Zeisler, U.S.A. The double weaves in center warp yarns are braided.

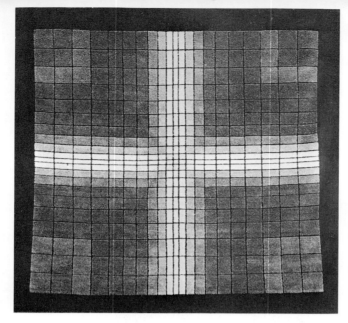

CROSS, by Noik Schiele, Switzerland. A knotted wall hanging, about 78" x 78", of silk and cotton, in green, blue, violet, and pink.

COMPOSITION IN BLACK, RED, AND BLUE, by Jan Hladik, Czechoslovakia. Gobelins technique, about 70" x 70".

Small window screen, by Ted Hallman, U.S.A. 30" x 50". The colors are reds and oranges; the round shapes are in solid acrylic, painted.

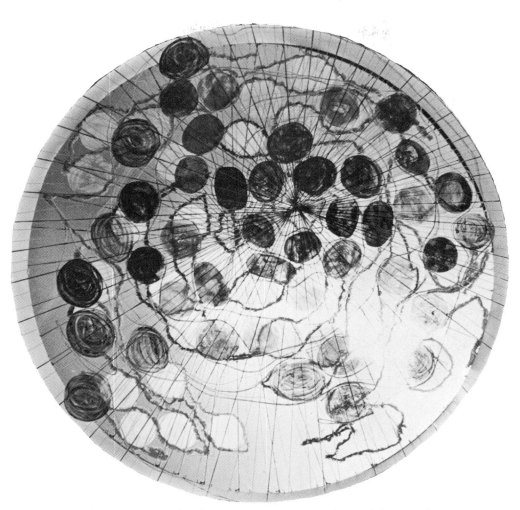

Circular screen by Ted Hallman, U.S.A. The screen, designed for a skylight, is 60″ in diameter. The colors are oranges, reds, blues, purples, greens, whites. Materials are wool, linen, cotton, steel, and vinyl. The round shapes are solid acrylic.

TULIP TIME IN MONSEY,
by Helen Kroll Kramer,
U.S.A. Wall texture, 27″ x
70″, in multicolored wool.
Photo by Eric Pollitzer.

HISTORIC OLOMONE IN THE NIGHT, by Jiu Fusek, Czechoslovakia. A tapestry, about 79'' x 79'', of wool. Browns, yellows, and white.

JOSEPH'S COAT, by Mark Adams, U.S.A. A tapestry,
66" x 72", of multicolored wool. *Photo by Skelton*.

Wall hanging, by Spencer Depas, Haiti. A macrame, 8' x 10', all of white twisted cord.
Photo by Monika Reichelt.

HOMAGE TO PAUL KLEE, by Esther Gotthoffer, U.S.A. A tapestry of mixed yarns.

Detail showing macrame knots of all-white wall hanging by Spencer Depas, Haiti. *Photo by Rosalind Depas.*

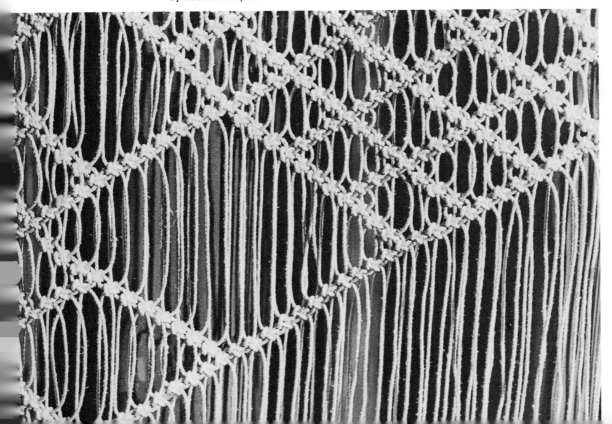

TROPIQUES, 1956, by Jean Lurçat, France. A tapestry about 126" x 266".
Photo by Galerie Pauli, Lausanne, Switzerland.

Opposite:
THE MIRACULOUS DRAUGHT OF FISHES, by Martta Taipale, Finland. A
tapestry of bright colors. *Photo by Kuva.*

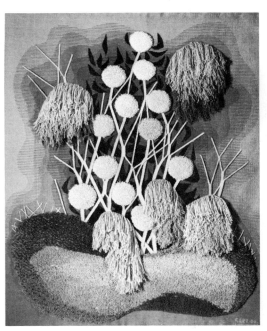

FLOWERS, by Luis Garrido, Spain. A tapestry,
48" x 60", of multicolored wool, in the Gobelins
technique and with knots.

THE POET, by Lenore Tawney, U.S.A. Black natural linen, feathers, wire. *Photo by Ferdinand Boesch.*

Part 2

The Art
of Weaving
Wall Hangings

Chapter 5
Equipment

Like the potter's wheel, which is the basic tool in the making of earthenware vessels, the loom of the weaver occupies a unique position in the handicraft arts. If the loom had never been invented, the craft of weaving would have followed a quite different course across the ages, and in the weaving of all textiles, including tapestries and wall hangings, there is no other article or equipment that is so indispensable.

In the selection of a loom there is one consideration that takes precedence over all others. It must be a good tool, so well constructed that it will not break down frequently and prove more of a handicap than an asset. Quality is of primary importance. Fortunately, there are many excellent home looms available, bearing the label of reliable manufacturers. There are many types of looms to choose from as well, but some are more practical than others.

Many minor technical limitations must be taken into consideration whenever a particular kind of weaving is contemplated, but the major concern is the actual width of the loom in relation to the finished material. It would be manifestly impossible, for instance, to make a wall hanging 60 inches wide on a 45-inch loom, unless the material is sewn together after weaving.

All the other considerations that must be kept in mind in choosing a loom will be discussed later in a special section. Here I have chosen only the six most important types of looms for detailed description. The first three are the typical tapestry looms, with the warp strung upright from top to bottom. On the other three looms the warp runs horizontally.

The first loom illustrated (Fig. 1) has an overall height of 54 inches and a weaving width of 35 inches. The roller beams, on which the warp is wound for transformation into the finished wall hanging is terminally equipped with steel ratchets. The weaver is thus enabled to wind long warps and make many wall hangings without continuously repeating the setting-up process. There is a single harness or shaft that slides forward and backward in grooves. On it there are strung steel heddles, and the threading procedure is quite simple.

One warp yarn is threaded through a needle eye, while the next and all of the following alternating yarns are guided through the heddles without being threaded. The threaded warp yarns remain in a fixed position, and sheds, or warp divisions, are made by moving the harness forward and backward.

Another loom, a considerably more advanced model (Fig. 2), has two harnesses that slide back and forth in a more purely mechanical way. They are operated by foot treadles, which produce perfectly tensioned sheds. This loom is also equipped with a beater that moves

efficiently up and down. The two solid beams are controlled manually to regulate the tension of the warp, which must be in accord with the various uses to which the loom is to be put. It is so versatile a model that it can also be employed in rug making, in which intricately woven designs play an equally important role. The weaving width of this treadle-operated loom is usually 45 inches.

The professional tapestry artist employs as a rule a tremendously large loom that is custom built. The Gobelins *haute-lisse* (high-warp) model is most often the loom of

Fig. 1 Upright sliding-harness loom built by E. B. Bosworth. From Shuttle Craft Guild Monograph 12, *Contemporary Tapestry*, by Harriet Tidball.

Fig. 2 Upright tapestry loom, 45" weaving width, from Nilus Leclerc Inc., Canada.

choice (Fig. 9). The sheds include both a shed stick and heddle bar, and the cloth beam is extremely large to prevent distortion of the rolled tapestry. The full-scale cartoon that is being copied remains on the wall, and the immediate part of the design is painted into the warp from a black-and-white original. Weft beating is done with bobbins or other appropriate tools.

Fig. 3 Small table loom, showing the beginning for a wall hanging.

The table loom is the smallest type of loom with horizontal warp weaving (Fig. 3). It is ideally suited for turning out quite small wall hangings, varying in width from 8 to 20 inches. A loom of this size occupies very little space, and is as easy to move about as a reading lamp or portable typewriter. It is especially valuable for sample making, and the creation of table mats

and other small home-brightening fabrics that nevertheless can be exceedingly colorful and enchanting.

The somewhat larger, 20-inch-wide floor loom (Fig. 4) takes up a little more space, but it makes weaving a great deal easier. To raise the harnesses for waft insertion or weaving, it is only necessary to push the treadles, which are connected directly to the harnesses. On such a loom one can weave a wide variety of tapestries, wall hangings, and practical textiles up to 20 inches in width.

The even larger floor loom (Fig. 6), which averages about 45 inches in weaving width, is perhaps the most versatile of all looms. It is particularly suitable for the decorative and dress fabrics that make the art of weaving much wider in scope than it would be if it were confined to the creation of wall hangings alone. This is a truly beautiful loom, fashioned of light wood, and so easy to operate that the additional space it takes up is something the purchaser will be very unlikely to begrudge. Its overall superiority more than offsets whatever small disadvantages it may possess.

To the beginner—and sometimes to the experienced craftsman as well—the choice of a loom may seem to involve many pitfalls. If a loom is very important to us, room in our homes can usually be found for it, even if it should be a large model and seem, at first glance, somewhat cumbersome. A very im-

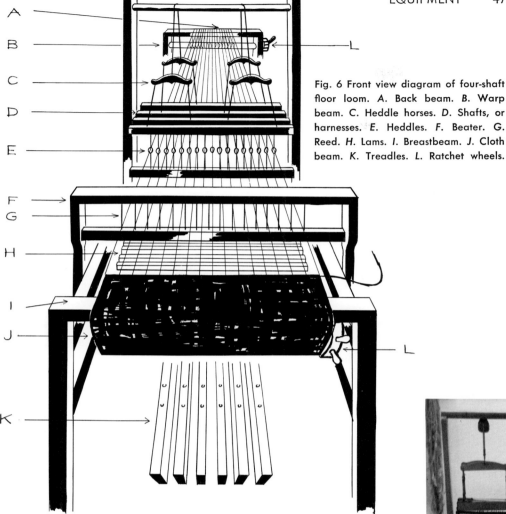

A
B
C
D
E

F
G

H

I

J

K

L

L

Fig. 6 Front view diagram of four-shaft floor loom. *A.* Back beam. *B.* Warp beam. *C.* Heddle horses. *D.* Shafts, or harnesses. *E.* Heddles. *F.* Beater. *G.* Reed. *H.* Lams. *I.* Breastbeam. *J.* Cloth beam. *K.* Treadles. *L.* Ratchet wheels.

Figs. 4 and 5 Two views of a modern floor loom, for 20″-wide wall hangings and other textiles. Four heddle frames suspended in the center from a crossbeam. Woven material is wound around front beam, and the warp around the parallel beam. Four treddles manipulate warp. *Photos by David Vestal.*

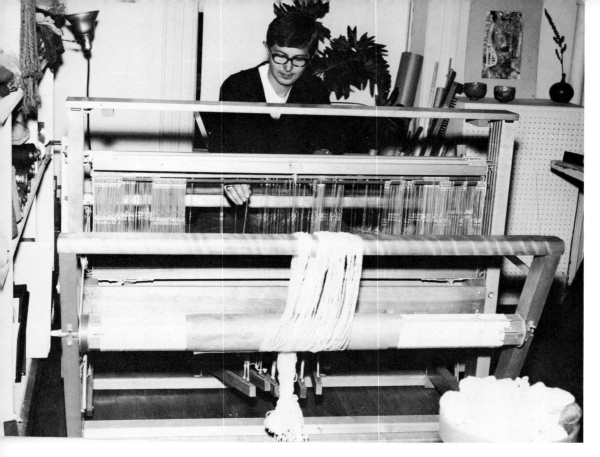

Figs. 7 and 8 Two views of jack-type folding loom 45" wide. This loom is equipped with a set of six treadles that equalize and centralize the weight of each harness, thus permitting the feet to be well placed on the pedals. It has rubber at its base, keeping it solid to the floor. It is equipped with the famous Leclerc automatic friction brake, always giving a perfect tension warp. From Nilus Leclerc Inc., Canada. *Photo by Len Depas.*

Fig. 9 Side view of upright loom—*haute lisse* (high warp). The outer frame holding the warp upright is of heavy wood. On the upper left are the width of warp yarns wound around a heavy roller, and for weaving space the unwound warp goes from top to bottom, held very tight by a large screw in the center. Behind the loom is the picture of the tapestry to be. Manufacture des Gobelins. *Photo by French Cultural Services, New York.*

portant factor, of course, is the price. But one can always begin with a secondhand loom, and the purchase of a new one can follow later. Actually, the cost of a good loom is seldom beyond the means of men and women whose incomes are distinctly on the modest side.

Personal preferences play an important part in the weaving of wall hangings. Some weavers are firmly convinced that such hangings cannot be made on low-warp looms; others have tried, and succeeded. But if one weaves only tapestries, and adheres to traditional techniques, it is advisable to own an upright loom. With the making of furniture fabrics as well as tapestries, a large horizontal floor loom becomes virtually a necessity.

Choosing a loom is very much like deciding on a car or typewriter or radio. When the field of choice is wide and there are many manufacturers competing, the advantage is always with the buyer who takes the trouble to become familiar in advance with the quality of a contemplated purchase. But in buying a loom the weaver's individual needs must be considered as well; and as weaving involves creative craftsmanship, these needs are certain to be highly variable.

In addition to the loom, the weaver will need several other articles of equipment. Some of these can be home-constructed. For the warp one must have either a frame (Fig. 11) or a warping reel to hold the yarns in tight consecutive order

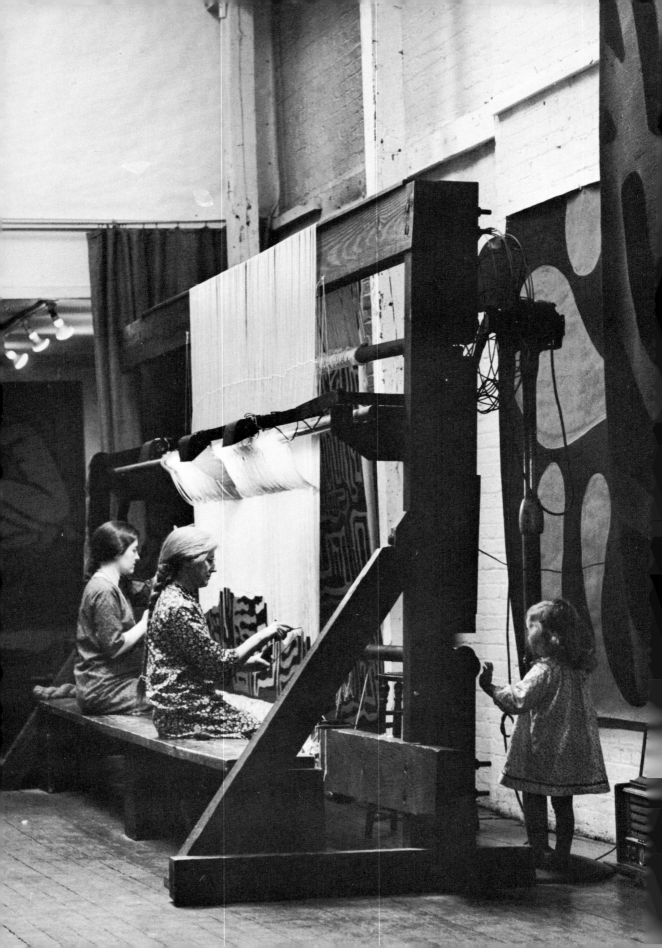

Opposite:
Fig. 10 Huge upright loom in New York Studio of Jan Yoors. Weaver on the right is pushing the weft yarn down into the warp. Behind the loom is full-size painting for the tapestry. *Photo by Jan Yoors.*

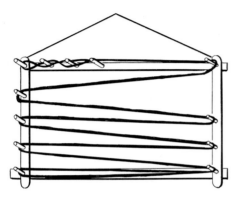

Fig. 11 Warping frame with yarns arranged crosswise.

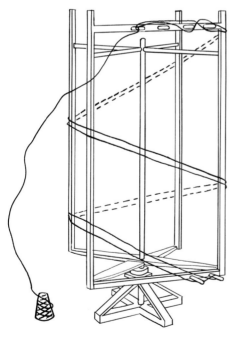

Fig. 12 Warping reel standing on the floor, with wound-around arrangement of yarns. One notation measures 3-yard length of warp.

(Fig. 12). The length factor is also of importance here. A warping frame is actually quite simple—almost exactly like a picture frame—and it is usually hung on the wall. It is furnished with pegs set at intervals of about 2 inches, along top and sides. The weaver fastens the beginning of the yarn on the first peg on the upper-left-hand corner of the frame. Then the thread is carefully guided across the frame and around the pegs, in a downward direction, until the desired warp length is obtained. The yarn is then led upward to the peg to which the yarn end was attached before it was drawn downward across the frame. This rotation is repeated until a desired number of continuous even lengths of thread are on the frame.

On small warping frames, only 5-yard warps can be made. On large frames, the number can be doubled. Small warping frames are used exclusively for short, narrow warps. The shortness of the pegs is so limiting a factor here that longer warps can only be made in sections, one section after another. More simply stated—and it needs to be stressed—the smaller warping frames can hold very little.

Although it takes up more space, a reel is much more convenient. Reel operation is similar to frame warping. A crossbar with four pegs is placed on top of the reel, and a yarn end is fastened around the first peg. When the warp cross has been arranged, the wheel is

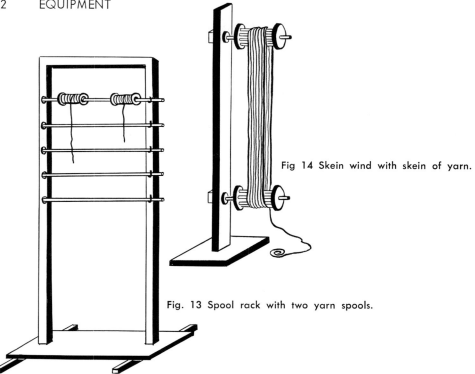

Fig 14 Skein wind with skein of yarn.

Fig. 13 Spool rack with two yarn spools.

turned by hand and the yarn is guided around the frame to the length needed for the warp. One rotation of the reel may measure out three yards. The yarn is then carried back around the reel to the peg on which it was first fastened, and the reel is turned back and forth until the required amount of yarn is ready to lift to the loom.

Yarn that is purchased for weaving purposes is almost always spool-wound, and these fiber or wooden spools can be easily slipped on the rods of a rack (Fig. 1). The racks, which may be purchased or home-structed, hold twenty to sixty spools, but more than eight spools are seldom required for a single warp. A rack like the one illustrated—a small upright frame with a few movable,

horizontal rods—can easily be made at home.

For handling skein or hank yarns a winder is used. The illustrated winder, which is about 4 feet in height, stands on the floor, and has an upright beam with two movable rollers (Fig. 14). The yarn is placed over the top and bottom rollers, which are adjusted in accordance with the length of the skein. The simple winding of yarn is the exact opposite of a complicated process, and for this purpose a chairback may also be used.

For making warps and filling spools a bobbin winder is absolutely essential. The bobbin winder in the accompanying illustration is securely attached to a table, and has a long spindle on which spools fit

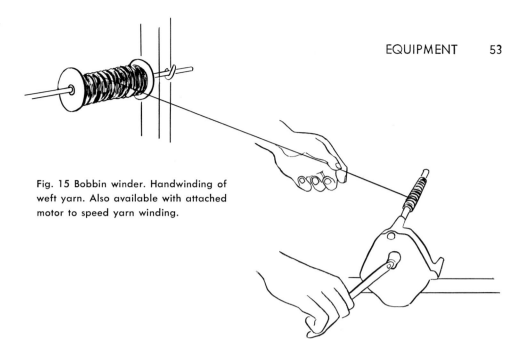

Fig. 15 Bobbin winder. Handwinding of weft yarn. Also available with attached motor to speed yarn winding.

tightly (Fig. 15). This winder is generally employed for winding yarn from a large spool or skein, onto a small weft spool or quill.

Yarns come in all lengths, colors, and quantities. The weaver quickly becomes an expert in skein identification, and here again personal preferences play an important role. But there is one procedure he must always follow. In preparing his threads he must rewind the skeins on spools or bobbins, in order to make them easier to handle.

Spools are used for warping— on frames or on a reel. For the wefts or filling, the weaver employs a wide variety of bobbins and shuttles (Figs. 16 and 17). The traditional tapestry weaver working on an upright loom uses all kinds of bobbins.

Fig. 16 Weft bobbins, or quills, that fit in the shuttle spindle on the quill at the right side of the illustration are made from paper or fiber.

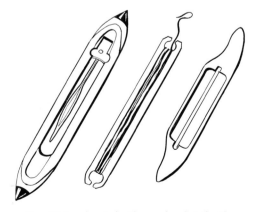

Fig. 17 Two boat shuttles and a flat shuttle (center).

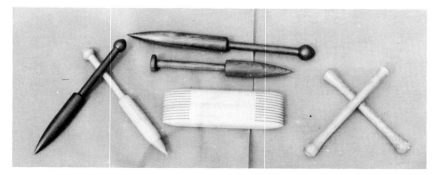

Fig. 18 At the upper center and left are Gobelins bobbins; on the right are two Aubusson bobbins. In the center is a beater, or comb, to push wefts together.

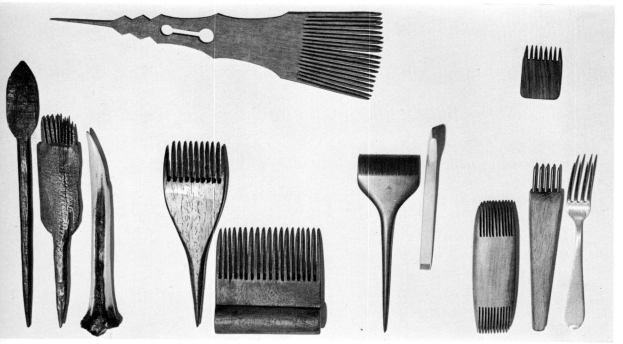

Fig. 19 Beaters. At the top of the photograph is a beater from Tanganyika, and, at top right, a small one from Sweden. Below, from left to right, are three from Peru, two Navajo, American Indian, beaters; two from Japan, with one lying on its side; one from Aubusson, one from the United States, and a table fork. From Shuttle Craft Guild Monograph 12, *Contemporary Tapestry*, by Harriet Tidball.

Fig. 20 Butterfly made from yarn lobe used for weft in weaving.

Some work with the Gobelins bobbin, which is about 8 inches in length, with a pointed pin-beater at the end. Half of this bobbin is covered with a wound-around yarn. The Aubusson bobbin bears a striking resemblance to a flute, for it is a thin, 5-inch spool that bulges at the ends, and sometimes has one flattened side to prevent rolling (Fig. 18). Weavers also make a rather unusual bobbin from the yarn itself; it looks like a butterfly. In the butterfly bobbin the yarn is wound over and around the thumb and little finger, and the beginning yarn is pulled from the inside (Fig. 20).

In the weaver's craft imagination and creativity walk hand in hand, and it is not surprising that bobbins should have acquired a measure of importance that makes them seem almost symbolical of the entire weaving process, for they are colorful objects indeed.

If the weaver works on an ordinary, low-warp floor loom, he does not, as a rule, employ the bobbins described above. He uses several other kinds, including the flat shuttles made from wool or fiber that are very convenient if many colors are needed. The smallest can be 4 or 5 inches long, and about an inch in width. The weft is wound lengthwise.

If one weaves at the distance of a yard lengthwise across the total width, a boat shuttle, in which a spool is attached to the spindle, is also used. The spools that are fitted on the shuttle spindle may be straight or tapered, and of fiber, wood, or plastic. They can be homemade from brown wrapping paper, and are cut oval shape, tightly wound and tape-sealed on the spindle of the bobbin winder (Fig. 16). The weft beater is comblike or forklike, and is used by the weaver to rake down the warp. An ordinary eating fork can be used for this purpose, but on the more modern type of loom the reed is the beater (Fig. 21). The comb, or reed, which is as wide as the loom, is enclosed in a wooden frame that is attached to the loom and is technically referred to as the beater.

Reeds are classified according to the number of dents they contain. A Number 10 reed, for instance, has ten dents, or openings, per inch. The choice of a reed depends on the density of a projected wall hanging. The most useful are numbers 10, 15, and 20. These descriptions of modern loom construction should make it fairly simple to comprehend the functions of looms and loom parts in current use. Understanding a loom and all its parts is essential, of course, to free and unselfconscious weaving.

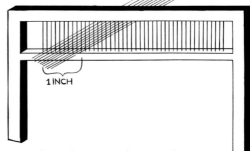

Fig. 21 Reed, in beater, with unit of ten dented warp yarns.

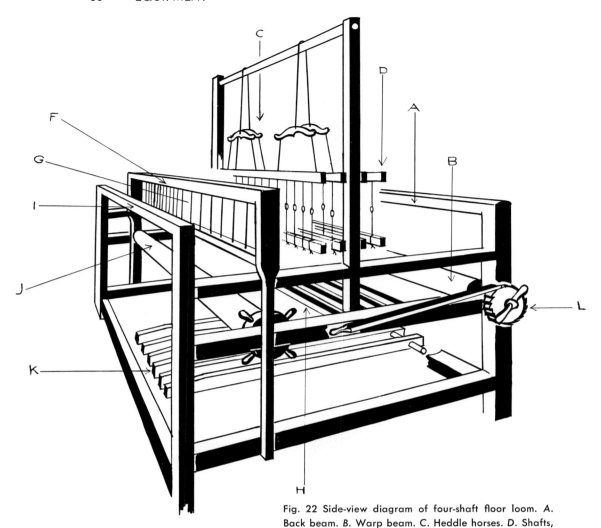

Fig. 22 Side-view diagram of four-shaft floor loom. *A.* Back beam. *B.* Warp beam. *C.* Heddle horses. *D.* Shafts, or harnesses. *E.* Beater. *G.* Reed. *H.* Lams. *I.* Breast-beam. *J.* Cloth beam. *K.* Treadles. *L.* Ratchet wheel.

PARTS OF THE LOOM AND THEIR FUNCTION

Contemporary looms are of every size—small ones for tables, and large floor looms. The basic parts of hand looms are similar, and differ chiefly in details of operation. Once we have acquainted ourselves with the essentials of a loom, handling will be easy.

Let us take, as an example, a loom diagram (Fig. 22). This one is of medium size and stands on the floor. Looms, like any other articles of furniture, are of different styles and are made of various kinds of wood, principally birch, maple, and walnut. The outer frame of our example consists of four upright posts connected by straight beams and forming a solid structure almost like a block.

In back of the loom is a large roller, the width of the frame. On this roller, or warp beam, the warp yarns are arranged side by side and wound according to the length of the intended cloth. The warp lines are then guided from the roller on the back and put through the handle frames hanging at the center of the loom. Finally the yarns are guided to the front of the loom, where they are wound on the front roller, under the breast of the weaver.

In the center of the loom, the harness frames (or shafts) hang from a superstructure built on the loom. Each shaft is an elongated frame with upper and lower strips of wood, connected at the sides with narrower metal strips. The pendant heddles are strung like an unbroken row of vertical wires on two rods fixed at top and bottom, inside the frame.

This lineup of vertical strips, which cut off the weaver's view through the loom, may be made of string, wire, or other metal. Each wire heddle has a loop at top and bottom that fastens to the horizontal metal strips at top and bottom, inside the frame. In the center of each heddle or string is an opening or heddle eye—similar to the eye of a needle—through which each warp yarn is threaded.

The loom has four shafts, each loaded with its heddles, through which will be drawn all the warp threads the weaver will use. The shafts, which hang behind one another, are parallel to the front roller, or breastbeam. So that warp yarns will run from back to front of the loom at a smooth, table-like level, the eyes of the heddles are at exactly the same level as the front and back crossbeams of the loom.

On this loom, as illustrated, the shafts are fastened with hooks and short cords to hanging mechanisms (heddle horses) that adjust each shaft according to required warp lifting for a pattern. The heddle horses look like small coat hangers, and the required number of shafts are hung from a series of these, suspended and clearing each other.

Each shaft is string-tied to the heddle horses from the superstructure or top beam of the loom. The number and grouping of shafts thus individually harnessed depends on the warp-lifting requirements of a specific weave design.

Immediately in front of the shafts and tall center structure of the loom is a swinging frame, the width of the loom and fitted with comblike wires. This is the reed, and the warp yarns pass through its openings, or dents. The function of the reed is to hold the warp yarns in place and at equal distances one from another. The reed tractions and governs the density of the warp threads after they have been passed forward from the heddle eyes. For example, if groups of ten threaded

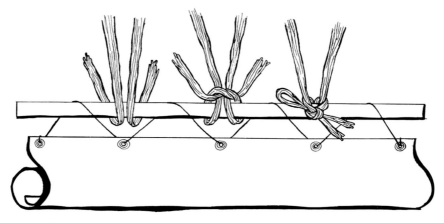

Fig. 23 Action of group tying of warp around rod.

warp yarns are to be equally spaced, one inch apart, a reed of ten openings per inch will be the spacing required. It is also possible to pass two threads through a dent, thus achieving twenty threads per inch, or a closer warp set.

The warp yarns pass from the dents of the reed at the top of the breastbeam, where they are group-tied around a rod parallel with the cloth roller. The rod is connected to the roller by a cord or other sturdy fabric (Fig. 23). On the loom a canvas is tacked along the cloth roller, around which it is wound a few times. The edge of the canvas, extending the full width of the breastbeam, is furnished with eyelets; these are laced to the rod with cord, as illustrated. The warp yarns are similarly attached to the warp beam at the back of the loom.

To tie the yarns, the weaver selects a small bunch of the warp threads that hang from the front of the reed. He divides the bunch in two parts and puts them over and around the rod, fastening them in a knot and half-bow. The process is repeated until all the yarns are tied to the canvas, or apron. After the warp threads are on, the harnesses are connected with the pedals.

Underneath the harnesses, at the center of the loom, are four long wooden rods, attached from the right, on the bottom of the loom frame. A rod, or stick, passes through holes in the lam, enabling them to move freely. The lams are the connecting link between the shafts and the pedals. Strings are used to tie the shafts to the lams and the lams to the pedals, which are long, flat pieces of wood attached to the crossbeam at floor level, under the back roller (Fig. 24).

In the illustrated example, each lam is tied with long string to a pedal. Then a longer string is looped through the ring and passed down the pedal, where it is connected to another ring screw. All of the lams are fixed to the pedals in this manner. When the weaver pushes down the left treadle, the front shaft will lower, while the others remain stationary. This is the operation that forms the opening, or shed, in the weaving process.

Weaving area is the space at the front of the loom between beater and breastbeam (Fig. 80). After a few inches of weft are interlaced, warp from the roller is brought forward by means of a ratchet wheel on the exterior—right-hand side—of the loom frame. A long stick, or pawl, screwed to the frame, between the cloth roller and beater fits into the pegs of the wheel. By pressing down on this stick, the weaver gradually advances the warp threads. A hand-turned wheel in the front roller is used for winding finished cloth. The ratchet wheels on the front and back rollers serve to maintain even warp-thread tension throughout the weaving process.

The loom shown in the illustration affords a good typical example of the parts and their tie-up and operation. The function of all looms is twofold. First, a loom must hold lengthwise yarns or warp in tension in such a way that groups of threads may be raised or lowered to accommodate the passage of weft. The other loom parts—reed, treadles, and the like—make weaving easier and speed production. The basic loom has never changed in its fundamental structure, but parts and improvements have been added for easier and better working procedures.

The width of looms varies from 8-inch table models to 80-inch floor looms on which two weavers work at the same time. A medium size—the 40-inch—is a large piece of furniture, made in different styles. Some of these are short in depth, and there are several folding models.

The choice of a loom depends, fundamentally, on the kind and width of material a weaver plans to use. The choice of a loom should also be guided by a little knowledge of varieties and kinds, so that a loom will be purchased that suits the weaver's taste.

THE COUNTERBALANCE LOOM

Hand looms are manufactured with three different harness-lifting devices: counterbalance, jack type, and counter-marche. The counterbalance loom is the easiest to operate. If the weaver requires two shafts up and down, he simply pushes the treadle to which the two down shafts are connected (Fig. 22). But since the shafts are permanently tied in groups at the top of the frame in counterbalance looms, and uneven—3 and 1—division of warp threads is difficult to achieve. This limitation can be overcome with a little experience in adjusting the shafts, and irregular weave constructions can be produced on the counterbalance loom.

Shaft and treadle hookup on this loom are quite simple. For example, if we have a pattern in which single shafts should rise in succession, only the following connections are made: To one treadle tie shafts 2, 3, and 4; to the next treadle, 3, 4, and 1; and on the third, 4, 1, and 2. On the last, or fourth, shaft tie 1, 2, and 3. Thus, with the first treadling, the first shaft is lifted, and in the following the remaining shafts come up, one after another. Using the counterbalance loom, the weaver needs to know only the shafts or warp threads that should remain down for this particular pattern.

THE JACK-TYPE LOOM

On the jack type each shaft operates independently, permitting both balanced and unbalanced weaves. Jack-type looms operate in reverse to counterbalance models. The treadles pull the shafts up instead of down—a result of the shaft-tying on top of the loom (Fig. 26). The mechanics are similar to those of a crane. When the weaver needs shaft 1 raised, he simply connects this shaft with the treadle.

THE COUNTER-MARCHE LOOM

Counter-marche looms combine the best features of the other two principal types. Using a double set of

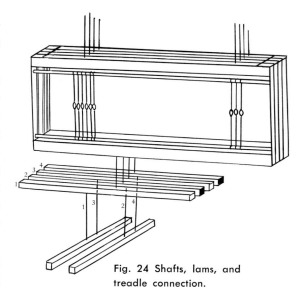

Fig. 24 Shafts, lams, and treadle connection.

lams, a good shed is created for uneven weaves. But a double set of lams requires double tying. If the weaver wants shafts 1 and 2 raised, he connects two strings from the lams that bring them up, and two strings from the lam set that lowers the other two shafts. Treadle action on this loom is not so easy as on the other types, since all the shafts operate together in one movement.

Large looms are most useful and pleasant to work on, but smaller sizes have many practical uses. On simple frame or primitive looms one can weave beautiful tapestries and learn a great deal about first principles in weaving. Small and primitive looms are cheap, too, and are ideal if one does not have space for the larger sizes. But on the small type there are no shafts or beaters, and the weaving is slower than it is on treadle looms. Also, width and length of material are limited—as was the case in primitive weaving. Nevertheless, one can make enough

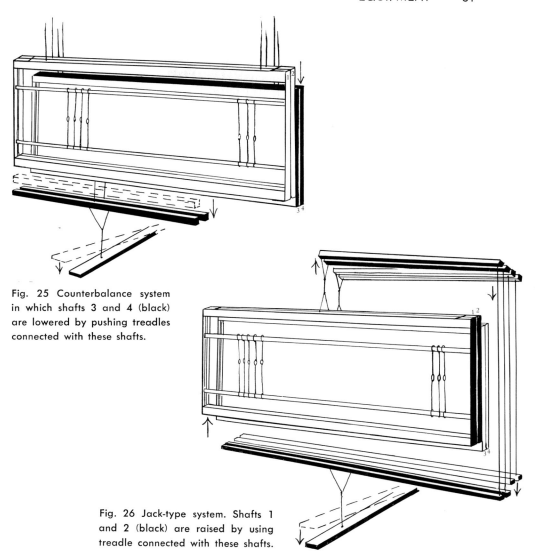

Fig. 25 Counterbalance system in which shafts 3 and 4 (black) are lowered by pushing treadles connected with these shafts.

Fig. 26 Jack-type system. Shafts 1 and 2 (black) are raised by using treadle connected with these shafts.

yardage for a handbag or belt on frame looms, and they are ideal for children and beginners.

Small table looms, which are models in miniature of the larger kinds, are the popular contemporary type of loom. These make cloth 8 to 20 inches wide, and have two to four heddle shafts and a beater. Weaving goes fast on a table loom, and the weaver creates larger pieces than he could on frames. By begin-

ning with a table loom he quickly and conveniently learns fundamentals. Table-loom operation is easy.

LOOM CHOICE

The majority of looms are in homes, because of the twentieth-century revival of interest in handweaving. Most often it is in the home that men and women discover fabrics, and develop their interest into a vocation and art expression. But a home loom must be as good as the commercial kind if student weavers are to get encouraging results. If the homeowner has room and money, he will buy a good large loom. A 49- or 50-inch type with four shafts and six or eight pedals is practicable. On this loom he can weave narrow and wide materials and also tapestries, suitings, and large decorative fabrics. And a well-constructed hardwood loom lasts longer than the small, lighter styles. On a sturdy, large loom any weight of material can be constructed, even rugs.

Or a home weaver can choose a smaller floor loom, which is, ideally, about 20 inches wide. A vast range of materials can be woven on a loom of this type—table mats, scarves, and belts. Small looms are most inspiring and useful in inventive and experimental projects. Besides, one can always weave small, effective pieces and sew them together as coatings, upholstery, and other useful and decorative materials. And sometimes it is advisable first to buy a small loom, just to practice designing, until one is ready and prepared to purchase a large one.

The little table looms are the least expensive of all, and may be chosen simply because they are portable and as easy to put away as a typewriter or record player.

The weaver who likes more to invent than to produce yardage will be happy and content with these practical little looms. And they are useful even if one owns a floor model, because on a table loom a designer can visualize his pattern and test the production of it before setting it up in large. For children of ten or twelve, table looms are certainly the best educational choice.

Today it is not infrequent for people to build their own looms or have them built according to specifications dictated by personal choice. Blueprints for the home construction of looms are available, and weavers who have time and patience will find a great deal of satisfaction in possessing a loom that they have made themselves.

The choice of school and occupational-therapy looms depends on space, budget, student age, and teaching objectives. In grade- and high-school workshops several different kinds of looms should be represented. In school weaving getting acquainted with the various uses of the loom and experimenting possibly toward other arts and crafts vocations is more important than yardage production. Therefore variety of equipment is ideal. And these looms should be good ones, in order to stand up under wear. Children and young people, beginning with frame looms, soon learn to use table and floor models. Wide variety of equipment is also commendable for art-school, vocational, and therapy classes, although in the last named the looms generally are chosen or made for specific purposes.

Chapter 6
Yarns and Other Materials

THE MOST IMPORTANT—FREquently the primary—source of design inspiration are the yarns and other decorative raw materials of the weaver's craft. In color, texture, and durability the range of choice here is so wide that the variety factor alone presents a challenge that can hardly fail to prove exciting. Our curiosity is instantly aroused by the way yarns differ in their origin and natural characteristics, and we would have to be unimaginative indeed not to want to know more about them.

The weaver designer is first of all interested in the natural surface of the yarn fiber, and the aesthetic possibilities it suggests. The look of wool, for instance, is soft, dull, even sometimes heavy, but—quite paradoxically—it radiates as well an exceptional kind of warmth. For this reason wool is just the right traditional material for tapestries. Mohair and alpaca, while similar to wool, have considerably more sheen, and sheen is another valuable quality in design.

When the artist weaves an extremely light and soft hanging, fine threads are of great importance. He should study particularly linens and cottons, as well as some of the newly invented man-made fibers. Generally, as in the case of silk, for instance, he will be guided chiefly by the fiber's appearance; its strength and durability will be of only secondary importance. Silk, in addition to being luxurious, is a strong fiber, with excellent tensile qualities.

Weavers who make a point of studying fiber qualities are constantly discovering new design purposes in them. It is the individual weaver's persistence in this respect that rewards him handsomely in inspirational dividends; and the more aware he is of this, the better craftsman he will be.

Cotton, in its raw stages, is dull and fluffy. It has none of the warm, heavy look we find in wool. But to the weaver who is constantly searching for new sources of inspiration, these light and airy characteristics can provide almost limitless opportunities for creative improvisation. He will personally discover in the material aesthetic possibilities that may seem at times to verge on the miraculous, for with experience and determination it is possible to

63

feel and see, in the dry stalks of a plant, fiber qualities that are unusual and promising.

Analysis and appreciation of the surface aspects of yarns is usually immediately followed by a detailed study of their construction. But this is not always of vital importance in the making of wall hangings. The weaver's chief concern here is to make sure that the tapestry will hang well and be of fairly long endurance. That does not mean, however, that yarn composition should, under any circumstances, be slighted or relegated to a position of minor importance.

In the study of yarn quality the degree to which the fibers are turned or twisted and the number of plies, or strands, in a yarn will be found to determine much of its character. Straight threads are traditional and are composed of a variety of twists and plies of one fiber. Even when the raw material is soft, hard twisting will form a stiff yarn and change the surface qualities of the basic fiber. In a very tightly twisted yarn, the surface structure is almost invisible. The number of turns per inch governs the tightness or hardness of a thread.

When loosely twisted cotton is used, in warp and filling, a smooth, dull appearance results. For a stiffer and more structural effect, a harder-twist thread must be used. Movement and design variation can be achieved merely by combining various twists of the same fiber in warp and weft. This is a reliable way to achieve texture without employing novelty yarns or complex weaves. When one desires to make a warp composed of bands of varying width, for example, six soft twisted threads should be chosen, and alternated with some harder yarns to create a pattern of verticals in a monotone tapestry.

The changes or variations that can be achieved in weaving a single straight thread fiber are numerous indeed, for by employing threads of different sizes, or plies, a great many additional patterns can be created. Greater contrast can be attained by simply increasing the length between yarn variations. This also produces a much more pronounced overall design. But it should be borne in mind that rhythm in a wall hanging depends on many factors. The weaver has a very large assortment of decorative materials to choose from, not the least exciting of which are beautiful fringes of many lengths and shades, embroidered trimmings, ribbons, and colored beads. Feathers have been used a great deal in South America and soft, decorative plumes of all sizes are becoming increasingly popular with weavers in the United States who are experimentally inclined. Some weavers are fascinated by the variety and bright, highly decorative coloration of seashells, but shells are extremely difficult to incorporate in a wall hanging. Dried flowers and leaves are more frequently used, and blend enchantingly with designs that suggest the changing seasons, from January snows to the opening buds of April and the russet-and-gold splendor of the autumn woods. A heightened enjoyment comes when you explore and discover, in Nature's prodigal wonderland, new materials that are excitingly different and have never been used before. The great variety of beads alone opens up fascinating avenues of exploration. There are round beads, large and small, made from wood, glass, or plastic. Then we have bead types in elongated and fancy shapes. One can naturally also paint the beads in appropriate colors before weaving. They can constitute part of the design. If you know a potter, he can make you a wide variety of beads or a great many large and small ceramic decorations. The field of ceramic decoration is comparatively new, and can open up a wide range of novel ideas.

Feathers in all lengths and colors have been used a great deal in Peru. The use of feathers in wall hangings is very much liked today. You might make a wall hanging in transparent leno technique, then tie in the feathers in a twisting of warp pairs. Just as with beads, dried flowers and leaves can provide an excellent point of departure when one wishes the weaving process to be highly individualistic.

There is also a wide assortment of seeds that can be used to heighten the beauty and originality of a tapestry. They can be either natural or painted. For instance, from gourds, peaches, avocados, and a number of other stones and fruits strikingly original wall hangings can be created. As soon as your artistic imagination becomes genuinely stimulated, you can work out your own special inventions, utilizing everything you may find suitable in your surroundings. Everyday materials can be used to excellent advantage if you have a bent for pop art. Cut out strips from fabrics and weave them into the warp. Leather, which comes in a great range of colors, can be cut into strips or motifs. You can paste ready-made gold and silver stars onto fabrics. These, too, add a touch of enchantment. The various dots that can be purchased in any stationery shop dealing in artcraft materials can be substituted for the stars or combined with them.

Christmas decorations should be collected for possible future use, for they are often unusual in design and provide scope for exciting experimentation. You can make a hanging with a combination of ribbons or gold and silver synthetic tape. Little glass balls add a touch of the exotic.

You can cut from cardboard large and small stars, and wind the yarns around them in do-it-yourself fashion. You can also paint the stars or paste the threads together. Today there are many pastes on the market that do not harm fabrics.

There are also bamboo sticks in a large assortment. They come in round shapes and can also be cut apart into flats. You can use them unpainted or color or stain them. Branches collected on a walk through the woods or pruned from plants in the home can be used to enhance the magic of a woodland scene in pictorial tapestries. Or go to a lumberyard, where you can get strips of wood in all widths and length, including a variety of wood shavings.

In the last two or three years some unusual new synthetic materials have become available. Plastic tubes can be incorporated with the narrow, flat yarnlike materials such as Mylar and Rovana. You can also purchase acetate in strips, and use them without alteration. Many artists cut out shapes from uncolored plastic materials and paint them before weaving. Every year sees an increase in the variety of both traditional and new materials available to the weaver.

Fig. 27 HISTORIC OLOMONE IN THE NIGHT (detail), tapestry by Jiu Fusek, Czechoslovakia. This work is made from wool, achieving the traditional smooth-all-over surface.

Fig. 28 Tapestry for the Grey Nuns Chapel in Montreal, by H. Riedl-Ursin, Canada. This modern tapestry is made from homespun wool and mohair. The use of this variety of wool types gives a contemporary look and irregular surfaces.

YARN

In the early development of weaving, before the advent of modern techniques had made many of the primitive procedures obsolete, long grass, rushes, and other plants were prepared carefully in advance of the actual weaving process by splitting and soaking. With the discovery of more and more materials that could be stretched and twisted in continuous threads, interlacing soon required less advance preparation.

Among the fibers most frequently spun into yarn are hairlike units of cotton and fleece, in extremely short lengths. Silk is much longer and straighter, for it is a filament that needs only to be unwound from a cocoon. The spinning has been done by Nature. Every textile has its specific use, and both short and long lengths serve as suitable yarns as weaving requirements vary. Strength is of paramount importance, for it is virtually impossible to turn a yarn that breaks easily into a satisfactory thread for tapestry making. As a rule long fibers make strong threads, and a cotton spun from long fibers is stronger than one made from shorter units simply because the fibers can be twisted together more often. It is of the utmost importance for the fibers to adhere together during the weaving process. The roughness of wool produces a pronounced resistance during spinning, and its fibers cannot easily be pulled apart when several units are twisted together. Silk and synthetics have as a rule considerably less resistance because of their smooth surfaces. There are many other qualities in fibers that must be taken into consideration, such as fineness, porosity, and stretchability.

The more pliable a fiber, the easier it is to manipulate, and very stiff fibers, such as jute, are not adaptable to spinning, unless they are to be used in heavy-grade projects. Linen is perhaps the sole exception, for it has qualities that counterbalance its stiffness. Fineness is of paramount importance in all weaving.

Porosity enables a fiber to absorb dyes and permit them to penetrate. In bleaching, a nonporous fiber is worse than useless. Conditions of wear to which the raw material will be subjected should be constantly kept in mind. A tapestry must be capable of withstanding the kind of wear that it is almost certain to be exposed to under the best of circumstances.

In commercial weaving the supply of fibers must be more or less regular. There are vegetable fibers that would be of great value for commercial use if they were less difficult to procure or less expensive, but the latter factor alone often prohibits their use in practical commercial weaves.

Finally, it should be borne in mind that natural fibers are directly derived from animal, vegetable, and mineral sources. The synthetics, on the other hand, are evolved yarns, and possess many quite different qualities. The common animal fibers are sheep wool and silk. The majority of vegetable yarns are spun from flax, cotton, hemp, and jute. Asbestos is a typical example of a mineral fiber that is often used in weaving. Silicates are employed in making glass threads. Among the more recent synthetic products are rayon, nylon, and plastic. All these fibers, whether natural or synthetic, must be processed before they can be converted into weavable yarn.

RAW WOOL

Wool, before it is processed, contains foreign matter, and is extremely dirty and greasy. It must be scoured in a water solution of soap and soda, and when it contains burrs and other vegetable matter this must be removed chemically by carbonization. New wools in many shades may be worked into attractive higher mixtures. Sheep fleece is no longer oily after it has been scoured, and it must be re-oiled before it becomes suitable for weaving. The shorter fibers are usually full of burrs, and cause great vexation to the operators of sorters and sorting machines. But usually burrs can be removed if sufficient persistence is exercised in that important stage of processing. All the foreign matter must be removed before carding to prevent injury to the machinery.

Fig. 29 Tapestry by Janice Bornt, U.S.A. In this 15″ x 17″ wall hanging, straight and flake yarns from wool and other raw materials are combined.

Fig. 30 RED CROCUS (detail), by Ann-Mari Forsberg, Sweden. The yarns are used in the traditional way from straight, smooth wool. *The Cooper Union Museum.*

WOOL CARDING

In wool carding, which includes the picking, teasing, and opening of fibers, a great deal or preliminary work must be done. Matted fibers must be disentangled and straightened. Before the picking machine was invented, this process was always done by hand. A traveling belt now carries the blended wool into a cylinder, and when the fibers have been mixed and made pliable the material is automatically passed on to the carder.

Three machines are customarily employed in this procedure. The group of carders, in the United States, are known as first, second, and third breakers.

Wool carding is a very ancient process, as old, in fact, as spinning. Sheepherders, both men and women, customarily took care of this procedure. Only the hand was used at first, but later a device for aiding the hand as a card was devised. It was made of wool or bone, and shaped like outstretched fingers. But today, of course, machines have completely replaced manual carding, and such primitive devices are merely of quaint historical interest.

WOOL AND WORSTED SPINNING

Coarse and smooth worsted yarns are produced by two different wool-spinning processes. The yarns are spun after carding, with no intervening procedures. Soft or slightly twisted strands are spool-wound and placed on a mule or ring-spinning frame. The fiber strands are then pulled tight, and if the material is not stock-dyed the yarns are wound into skeins or hanks on a swift.

The worsted variety of wool yarn involves the combing of the slivers before they are twisted into even and lustrous threads.

A number of slivers are drawn out, and the fibers are arranged in parallel fashion in a process called "gilling."

Worsted spinning is carried on by two systems. In the Bradford, or English, system long lengths of fine wool create an ideal yarn for suiting, since it is extremely lustrous in appearance. French, or dry, spinning makes use of shorter and less oily fibers, and produces soft but dull yarns. There is far more twisting involved in the Bradford system. The winding process follows immediately after spinning, and the spools of yarn are then ready for weaving, dyeing, and plying.

Fig. 31 NATURE AT NIGHT, by Lili Blumenau, U.S.A. Straight and handspun Haitian yarns of wool, cotton, and linen in fine and heavy threads are combined. *Photo by Spencer Depas. Collection, Lili Blumenau.*

Fig. 32 FLIGHT OF ANGELS, by Mark Adams, U.S.A. The desired effect is achieved with the traditional French wool. *Photo by Skelton.*

Fig. 33 WHITE IRIS, by Mark Adams, U.S.A. This tapestry is made with traditional straight wool.

MOHAIR

There are many other animal fibers besides wool that are extensively used in weaving. Mohair comes from Angora goat fleece. It has an average fiber length of from 9 to 12 inches, and is extremely long and curly. Turkey supplies the major part of this raw material, but there are Angora goat farms in Texas and other parts of the United States. Mohair is superior to sheep wool in some respects. It is extremely lustrous and elastic, and lends itself well to dyeing. It does not wrinkle to anything like the extent that wool does, even when it is many times folded. It is widely used for upholstery and tropical suitings and neckties. Colors show up well on mohair, and brilliant shades stand out strikingly.

CAMEL'S HAIR

Camel's hair has excellent textile qualities. Most of the raw material comes from Mongolia. Everyone is familiar with the camel's hair overcoat, of a vibrant tan color, which—until recently perhaps—was so much favored by American men, particularly by those in the theatrical profession. Camel's hair has insulating qualities that make it an ideal cold-weather garment.

SILK

Commercially, silk is the most highly favored material of the textile industry. It surpasses all other fabrics in brilliance. It has an interesting history. Thousands of years ago perhaps—although there is no certainty as to the exact date—the Chinese discovered how durable, as well as beautiful, was the thread spun by the larva of an Oriental moth. The discovery remained a carefully guarded secret until the fifth century of the Christian Era, when the Japanese turned the raising of silk-spinning moths into a preindustrial enterprise that soon spread to the Western world. It is thought that the Emperor Justinian was the first to have smuggled out of China the worms that brought silk into European history. There are three processes in silk production: sericulture, worm raising and selling of cocoons; reeling, the unwinding of cocoon silk into skeins; and throwing, the twisting together of two or more filaments.

Sericulture is most interesting. It cannot be undertaken in cold climates, and the work involves the expenditure of a great deal of patience. A silk moth's life is very brief, and it passes rapidly through three stages—that of the egg, the worm, the chrysalis, and finally that of the adult moth. First a large number of the worms are collected on a sheet; then they are washed in warm water and kept for a few days in a damp atmosphere before being put in cold storage. They remain under refrigeration until the mulberry season, when they can be assured of a plentiful supply of food. The freshly hatched silkworm is about ⅛ of an inch long. But its appetite is voracious, and it soon consumes 50 or 60 times its weight. When it is fully mature, it measures 3 inches in length.

The quality of the silk depends upon the mulberry leaves, and they must be selected with great care. When the animal is ready to spin, it announces its intention with a curious movement of its head, which resembles the figure eight. As soon as the glutinous fibers of silk are ejected from two openings just under its mouth, they harden into a single fiber. The worm goes on spinning until its supply of silk is exhausted. It then changes into a chrysalis and finally into a moth. When the time to emerge from the cocoon arrives, it moistens the end with silk and makes its escape.

In the production of raw silk the chrysalis is killed by heat, to prevent the moth from developing and destroying the silk. It is the wasted cocoon that provides the material for spun yarn.

RABBIT WOOL

This material is extremely fluffy and light, and is much favored by commercial weavers. When combined with other fibers it makes yarn fabrics that are soft, lustrous, and of very great beauty.

Fig. 34 Cotton plant at harvesttime. Cotton in its raw stage is soft and fluffy. *Natural Cotton Council of America.*

VEGETABLE FIBERS

Cotton is the most important of all the vegetable fibers. Cotton fabrics clothe most of the world's population, despite the wide use of other vegetable, animal and, recently, plastic materials in the production of wearing apparel. Cotton is grown in many countries throughout the world, but the United States and India are the foremost cotton-producing nations. The cotton shrub is 3 to 6 inches high, and its blossoms develop into a seed-bearing boll that contains an accretion of the fibers used for yarn.

Cotton picking is customarily done by hand, since it is hard to mechanize and the picker must constantly discriminate between ripe and unripe bolls. A more successful harvester than the men, women, and children who work in the fields, often for long hours and little pay, has yet to be invented.

Fig. 35 Detail of a tapestry made by a Lili Blumenau student. The soft cotton yarns are combined with other threads to achieve pronounced yarn effects. *Photo by Rudy Bleston.*

Ginning is the first step in the preparation of raw cotton for spinning. It cleans and separates the fiber from the seeds and the lint substances that adhere to it. The quality of cotton depends as much on careful ginning as it does on skillful picking.

When the material arrives in bales at the mills, it is still far from completely cleaned, and considerable dirt adheres to it. There are many fibers that must still be untangled, and further processing is necessary.

When cotton is placed on the open market, standards of grade and color are important factors in determining the price at which it is to be sold. Great stress is placed on such factors as uniformity, strength, smoothness, and silkiness.

Cotton spinning is a many-stage process, and as exacting as the spinning of wool or linen. As soon as the tightly packed bales are opened, the fiber is carried to a breaker on a traveling belt, where the individual fibers are opened and mixed with other fibers of the same length, or staple. When this is accomplished, the process continues in other machines, which are called pickers. Here the cotton is further opened and processed, so that adhering leaves and dust may be completely eliminated.

Each step further cleans, separates, and develops the raw material. The cotton card resembles the one used for wool. It consists of flat bars with teeth, and is attached to a continuous chain that passes over a cylinder that also has teeth. Here the last strands of poor fiber are separated from the good cotton.

Cotton is combed when fine grades of yarn are desired. This is done by means of selected slivers from the card that are united by the machine and fed to the comber, which in turn extracts all the remaining impurities. The combing procedure is repeated until the slivers acquire a lustrous softness.

LINEN

Linen comes from the flax plant, which was grown throughout the ancient world, particularly in Egypt. Today flax is mostly grown in Ireland, Belgium, and Germany. Linen weaving is a rather exacting process, for it requires an atmosphere in which the warp yarns can be kept constantly moist. The preparation of linen for the loom involves bleaching, starching, washing, beetling, and calendering. The final finish is by hydraulic pressure. Linen varies greatly in quality and texture, and skillful finishing enhances its appearance. It is one of the three or four most important weaving fabrics.

Opposite:
Fig. 36 LEKYTHOS, 1964, by Lenore Tawney, U.S.A. The woven form is in very light linen yarns. *Photo by Ferdinand Boesch.*

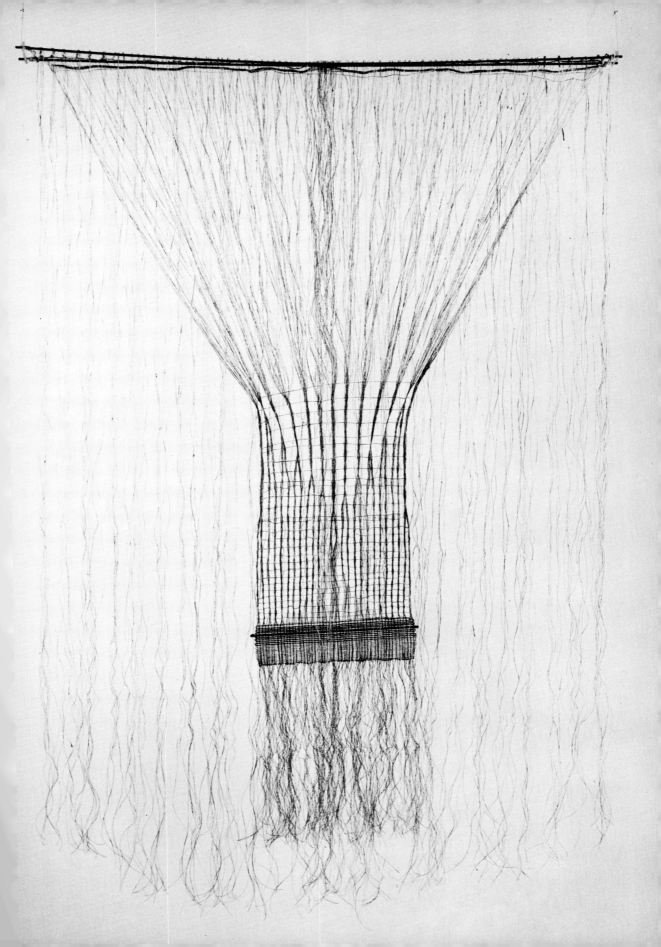

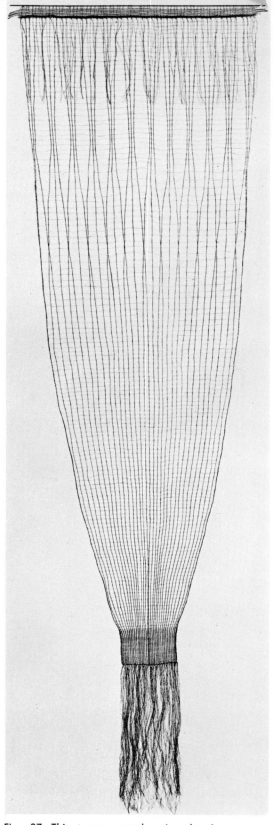

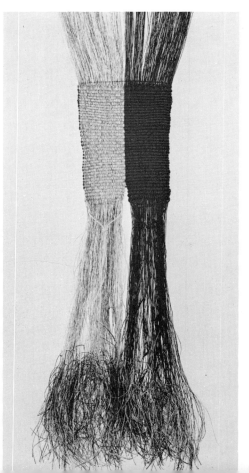

Fig. 37 This transparent hanging by Lenore Tawney, U.S.A., is made from fine natural linen. *Photo by Ferdinand Boesch.*

Opposite, top:
Fig. 38 The top of this wall hanging is used artistically by Lenore Tawney. The fine linen yarns are unwoven, then gathered together, forming part of the composition. *Photo by Ferdinand Boesch.*

Opposite, bottom:
Fig. 39 Bottom of above wall hanging is related to the upper part. Here again Lenore Tawney gathers fine linen with heavy weft yarn.

Fig. 40 MILLE FLEURS, a wall hanging by Ted Hallman. The artist cuts shapes from hard materials such as acrylic and Bakelite. Warp yarns are in fine linen.

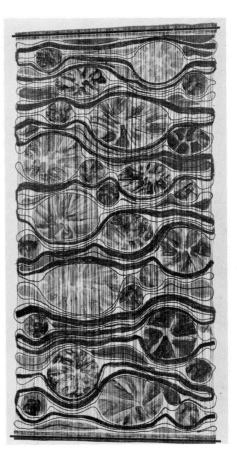

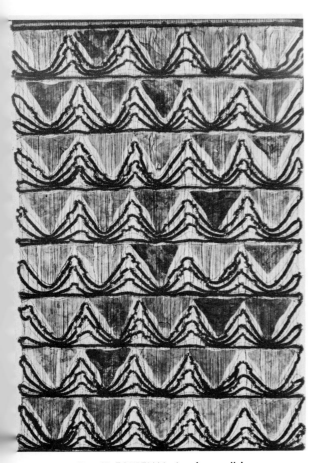

Fig. 41 EGYPTIAN. Another wall hanging by Ted Hallman, with cutout shapes woven into a fine linen warp.

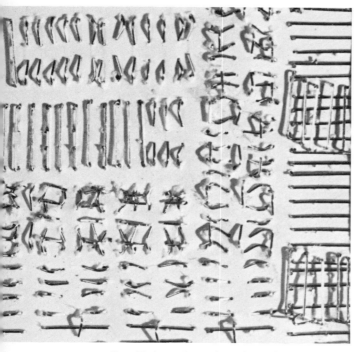

Fig. 42 A textile study with staples made by a student in the Lili Blumenau weaving workshop. Its purpose is to gain greater sensitivity for yarns and textures. *Photo by Rudy Bleston.*

Fig. 43 In this texture study, leaves from tobacco plants are flattened to form the background. Motifs are from small curved leaves. Thus a student at the Lili Blumenau weaving workshop achieves smooth and rough textures similar to the appearance of yarns. *Photo by Rudy Bleston.*

JUTE

Jute has been largely used in the past for the cheaper kinds of textiles, but in recent years it has come into more favor with commercial weavers because of its widespread use in upholstery. The plant is grown in China and in India. Carpets and burlap coverings are made of both fine and coarse jute yarns. The coarse yarns are the easiest to dye, but they wear less well and have a tendency to fade.

ARTIFICIAL FIBERS

More and more these are coming into common use. Modern laboratory research has contributed greatly to this development. Indeed, its effect has been to elevate the artificial above the natural and make it more sought after by weavers in general. More profit can be derived from an article when it is mass produced, because the production costs are not nearly so great. Luxury goods in natural materials have a price range few can afford, and it is a well-known fact that a demand for goods can be created where none has previously existed.

Many artificial fabrics are peculiar to the twentieth century, and some have been invented as recently as the past ten years. The first man-made fiber was designed to imitate silk. Rayon, or artificial silk, was first developed in Europe before the turn of the century, and the first rayon plant in the United

States was built in 1910. Designed at first solely to replace silk, it has since created a flourishing market of its own. The newer synthetics—nylon, Dynel, and Orlon—although they are advanced products of modern scientific research, seem unlikely ever to replace rayon, even though it has never altogether taken the place of silk, and the other natural fabrics it was designed to imitate.

NYLON

Nylon was among the first of the newly discovered synthetic fibers, and still remains perhaps the most important one. Research by Du Pont led to its discovery before World War II. Chemically, nylon is an amide. Its main ingredients are carbon, nitrogen, oxygen, and hydrogen. It is stretched considerably during the spinning process, and its molecules, or structural elements, are oriented in the direction of the axis, precisely as are fibers in worsted or combed cotton. In a way, it is a miracle fabric, for it is very strong, and has some of the characteristics of natural fabrics. It has won the place previously occupied by silk in women's hosiery.

PLAIN AND NOVELTY-TYPE YARNS

The weaver's raw materials are commonly divided into "plain" and "novelty." A plain thread is straight, but a novelty may be uneven or

Fig. 44 Heavy rope is used, plied, and taken apart to create another textile study by a student. Lili Blumenau weaving workshop. *Photo by Rudy Bleston.*

Fig. 45 Woven surface effects with plain and nubby yarns. Detail of a sample made by a student at the Lili Blumenau weaving workshop.

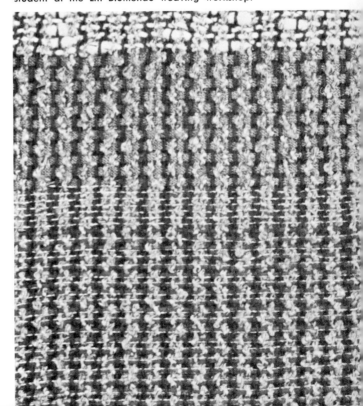

possess nubs or other fancy compositions. A great deal of weaving is done with single, plain yarn, but almost as often two or more singles are combined in a ply. There are also different kinds of yarn twists. In some fabrics loosely twisted thread is desirable, and in others hard twists, of which crepe is a good example.

YARN NUMBERING

Yarns are fine, medium, and coarse, and a numbering system has been developed based on pound in relation to yarn length, because manufacturers have to have a ready reference table that will enable them to know the quantity needed. Each material has its specific yarn count. The higher the number, the finer the thread. Number 1 cotton, for instance, is based on 840 yards per pound. There is no system for novelty yarns, since the length of these yarns depends on the thread design.

EXAMPLES OF COUNTS

Cotton

No. 1—840 yards per pound.
No. 2—(twice No. 1) 1,680 yards per pound.
No. 50—(50 times the amount in No. 1) 42,000 yards per pound.
The number 40/2 in cotton means two threads of No. 40 twisted together. The weight of two No. 40 yarns equals the weight of one No. 20 yarn of the same length. Or, 40/2 is equivalent in weight to 20/1 : 20 times 840 yards equals 16,800 yards per pound.
Number 60/3 cotton, for further example, is three threads of 60's, equivalent to the weight of one thread of 20's (No. 20/1).

Wool

No. 1—1,600 yards per pound: in woolen yarn, which is not plied.
In worsted yarn, No. 1 is 560 yards per pound. No. 2 worsted is 560 times 2, or 1,120 yards per pound. Number 40/2 worsted is equal to 20/1 in yards per pound.

Bast Fibers

No. 1—300 yards per pound: bast yarns generally are single, not plied.

Spun Silk

No. 1—840 yards per pound.
For spun silk single yarns, the cotton count is used; for the plys, a different count.
Example: a 20/2 spun silk is not two ends of 20, but two ends of 40, and has the same weight as 20/1.

Silk and Rayon

Silks and rayons are not counted in terms of pounds, but in deniers, a French measure of 4.464, or 528 yards per pound. Silk and rayon dealers provide charts in which weight and length are specified.

NOVELTY YARNS

Traditional weaving style ordinarily consists of representations in plain natural yarns. The modern tendency is to stress simplified geometrical and all-over structures that demand special yarns. Effect, or novelty, threads are produced in wool, cotton, rayon, and a number of other materials. A few novelties are made entirely of natural fibers. Most, however, are complicated styles, combinations of natural and synthetic materials, suitable for contemporary uses. The production of these fancy yarns varies, depending on current fashions. As a rule, the fancier yarns are made in coarse numbers, owing to the fact that their structures are elaborate.

There is no uniformity in novelty-yarn names, which makes it difficult to identify them. We can, however, describe the appearance of the more typical ones.

FLAKE YARN

These popular threads are single and plied. A single flake yarn is composed of fragments spaced on a basic thread, or consists of full portions tapering into thin and enlarging again to form thicknesses, or flakes. The flakes are often unevenly spaced throughout the threads. The twist given in spinning has a tendency to affect the thin parts, and therefore a great many more turns per inch are found in the thin portions than in the flakes. These yarns can be made from fibers of comparatively short lengths, which lend themselves to accurate turning. Most single flake yarns are cotton or staple rayon.

There are several varieties of plied flake yarn. Sometimes in this type a single flake yarn is combined with ordinary straight thread: a cotton flake with rayon binding, for instance. The fancy part may also be a different color from the binding. More unusual combinations consist of two single flakes or a ply flake twisted with ordinary two-ply yarn. When the single flake is combined with an ordinary thread, the two are usually twisted in opposite directions; thus the ply yarn becomes harder and shorter. This process transforms the soft, long flakes into bead effects.

NUB YARN

When fine lumps of short fibers are introduced in a wool or cotton yarn during spinning, nub yarn is created. These yarns are single or may be twisted with regular threads. Wool is the most adaptable material for this novelty. The nubs, which, as a rule, are in contrast to the ground thread color, are composed of fibers crossed in all directions, and introduced during carding. Unlike flake yarns, the added particles are unevenly spaced and simply laid and turned on the ground thread. Nub yarn is much used in weaving fancy woolen fabrics.

Fig. 46 NOVELTY YARNS

SINGLE FLAKE   FLAKE PLY   FLAKE PLY   NUB

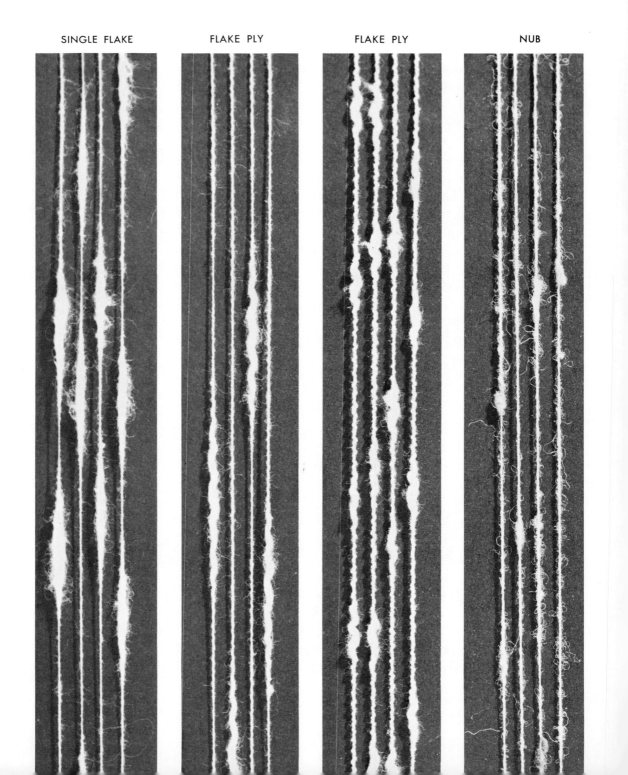

KNOP   LOOP   SPIRAL   RATINÉ

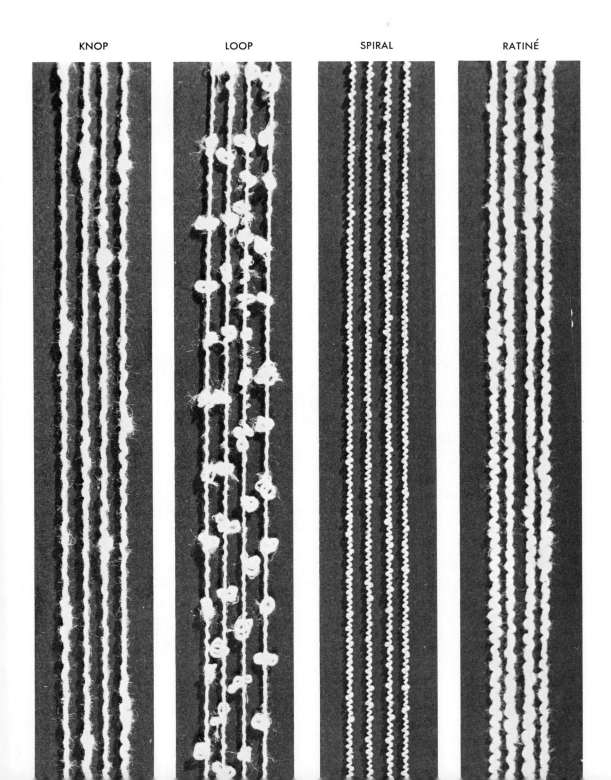

KNOP YARN

Knop yarns often are confused with the nub styles, perhaps because of the similarity of their names. However, a knop yarn has really hard knots, or particles of hard, twisted thread, quite unlike the soft, short bits in nub yarn. When two or more ground threads are twisted in the construction of knop yarn, one thread is released slowly and intermittently, the other rapidly and continuously. The faster-turning thread forms bunches called knops.

The hard knop occurs in different shapes, and the yarn is characterized by extreme contrast between knops and basic thread. The knops slide readily along the yarn, and therefore a thread—often of contrasting color and fiber—is twisted around the knop to prevent sliding. This design is called knotted twist. It is the most usual knop type, and the protective thread is strong, which helps in passing the yarn through harness and reed.

Fig. 47 Palm leaves, Egypt, Late Dynastic period, *The Metropolitan Museum of Art.* Palm leaves are still used in weaving, particularly in South America and the West Indies.

LOOP YARN

Wool and rayon loop, or curly, yarn is another one of the popular novelties. Its manufacture is similar to that of the knop and nub varieties. The binder ends are twisted in the usual manner, but a third end is let off in jerks during twisting, to form kinked and curled loops at regular intervals.

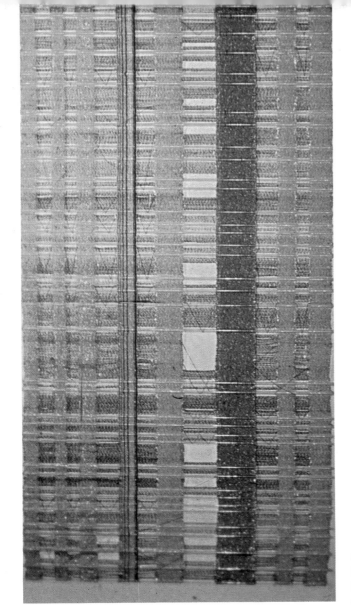

STRIPES IN MYLAR AND
PLASTIC by Lili Blumenau.
Detail below. *Photo by Len
Depas.*

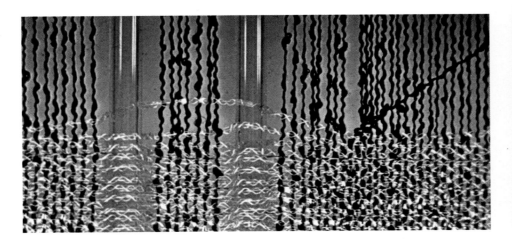

Wall hanging with leno by Spencer Depas of Haiti.
Photo by Len Depas.

BLACK CROSS by Spencer Depas of
Haiti. *Photo by Len Depas.*

SPIRAL AND RATINÉ

Spiral yarns consist of two single ends twisted—one delivered faster than the other, and wound around the more slowly rotating thread. Sometimes a hard-twist single and one softer single are turned together, or a thick and thin are combined. Spiral yarns of many colors and variations are produced by these principal methods.

Ratiné yarn is composed of a fine single thread combined with two-ply twisted yarn, the second twist opposite the first. The twisting opens the spiral yarn in a softly linked chain. Ratinés are cotton, spun rayon, and worsted. The spiral yarns are usually cotton or rayon.

CHENILLE AND OTHER NOVELTIES

Chenille yarn is not twisted. It is a thread that has been cut from woven goods in yarnlike textured strips. In weaving the material from which chenille is made, four to eight warp ends are spaced an equal distance apart, woven with heavy filling in plain weave or leno. After weaving, a machine cuts the filling between the woven strips, thus producing a thread highly suitable for hand weavers' designs.

Novelties can be varied—that is, they can consist of two kinds combined. Contrasts of color and raw material also play a pronounced part in the creation of effect yarns.

Light and dark threads, for example, may be used in twists of ratiné and flake, or a cotton base used with rayon binders. Gold and silver thread, split bamboo, ribbons, raffia, and many other materials are marketed for weavers to experiment with in new creations.

DYEING RAW MATERIALS

There are various methods of applying dyes to weavers' raw materials. Coloring raw fiber is called "stock dyeing." Yarns are also dyed after spinning, in accordance with the proposed design. The kind of dye used depends largely on the effect desired, as well as on cost.

STOCK DYEING

Wool, cotton, rayon staple, and waste silk may be colored in the raw stock. This is done in a rotation cylinder in which the fibers circulate in a dye bath. In another type, a cylinder is packed with the fiber stock and immersed in a dye tank. The revolving cylinder forces the liquid through the stock.

SKEIN DYEING

In this method the skeins, or yarn hanks, are hung on rods in a machine containing the dye liquid. The rods are revolved and submerged with the yarns in heated dye.

COP DYEING

Yarns from the spinning frame are sometimes wound on perforated spools and spindles and placed in a dye bath, the liquid circulating through the yarns. This type of dyeing also is done with warp threads on perforated beams. These are the chief dyeing methods, but there are many others.

Some artist-weavers do their own dyeing at home. In this case it is advisable to obtain dyes in powdered form; these are readily available. Here you have the advantage of mixing dyestuffs to obtain precisely the shades you want. However, because room to house the equipment, as well as space for drying the yarn, is necessary, home dyeing is usually feasible for weavers who live in the country. But yarns in numerous beautiful shades may be obtained from many sources throughout the world, thus permitting the artist to conserve his time for weaving.

Fig. 48 Wall hanging with dried flowers (detail), by Luella Williams, U.S.A. For the top, the weaver uses a tree branch. *Photo by Marion Wesp.*

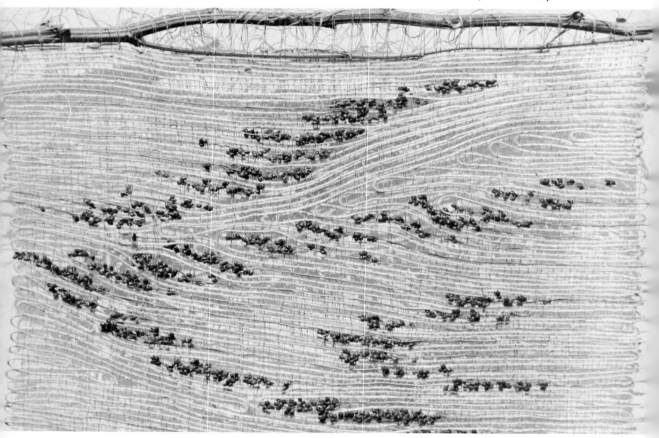

Fig. 49 Wall hanging (detail), by Luella Williams, U.S.A. A piece of bark and dried flowers are woven into a fine yarn warp. *Photo by Marion Wesp.*

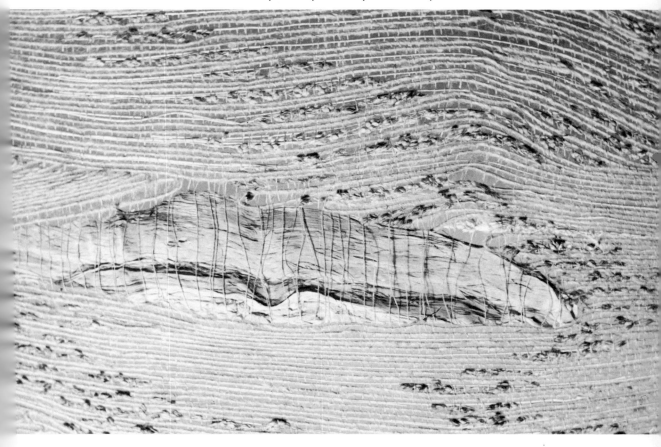

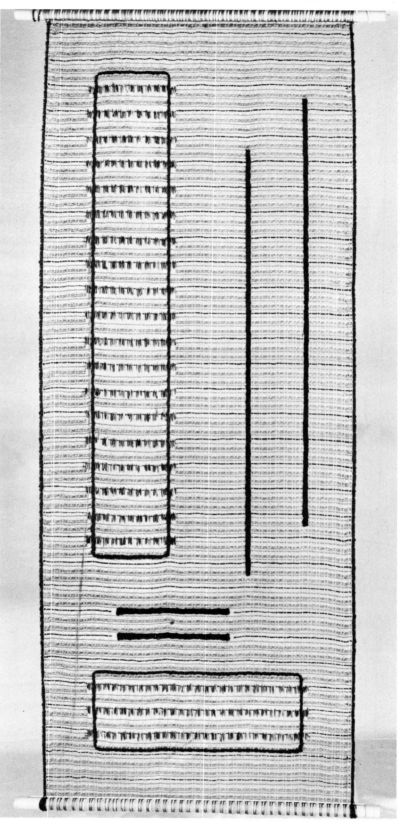

Fig. 50 Panel with gourd seeds, by Evelyn Gulick, U.S.A. Warp is in natural and brown linen. Gourd seeds are strung on linen yarn. *Photo by Harry Crosby.*

Fig. 51 Panel with gourd seeds (detail), by Evelyn Gulick. Here one can see clearly the strung gourd seeds. *Photo by Harry Crosby.*

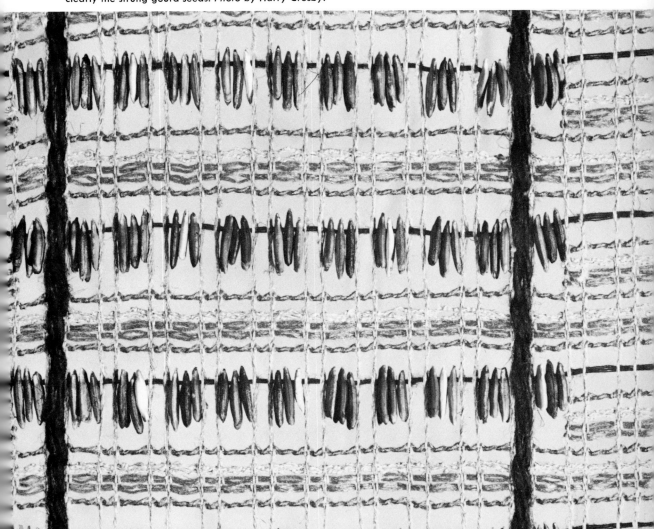

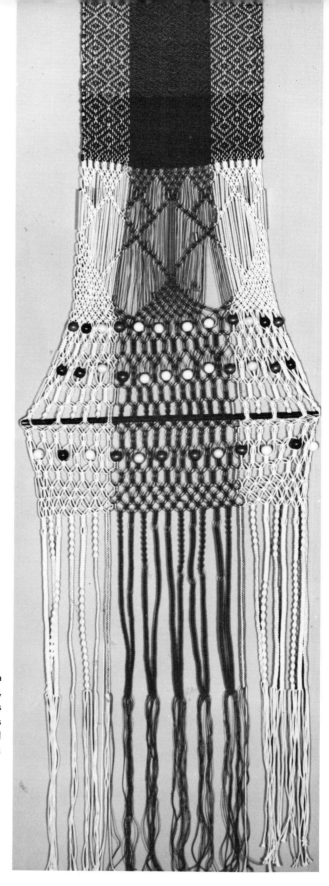

Fig. 52 In combination with weaving and macrame, Spencer Depas, of Haiti, uses large round wooden beads in yellow, red, green, and blue. Macrame knotting is from cotton twine.

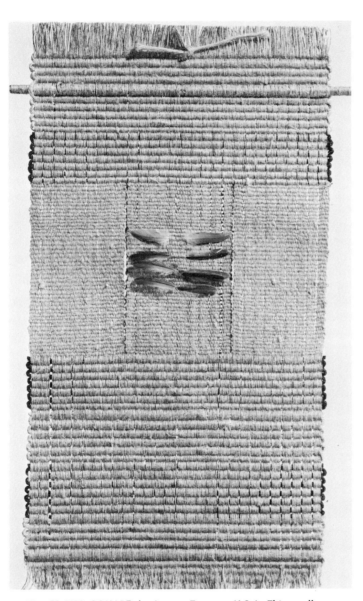

Fig. 53 BIRD SQUARE, by Lenore Tawney, U.S.A. This small wall hanging is very closely woven in linen; feathers in the center form the motif. *Photo by Ferdinand Boesch.*

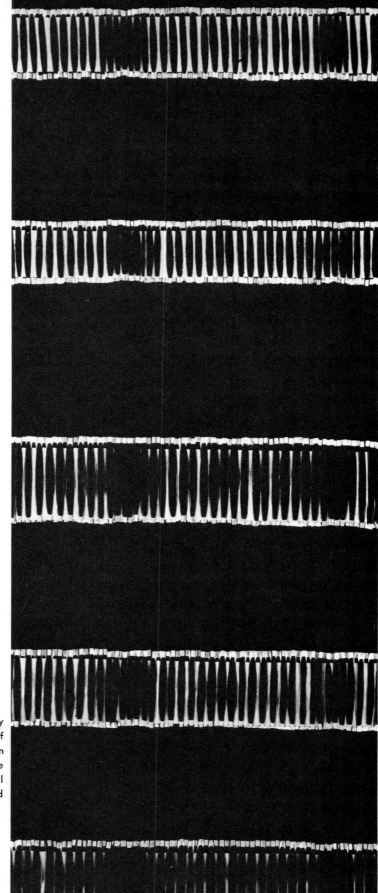

94

Fig. 54 Wall hanging, by
Erica Kluger, Israel, of
wool and raffia. The open
parts, or bands, are
finished with white metal
and inlaid with gold
leather.

Fig. 55 Wall hanging (detail), by Erica Kluger. White metal and gold leather are effectively used.

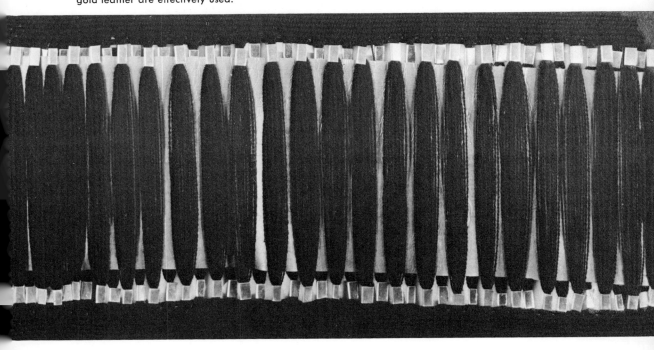

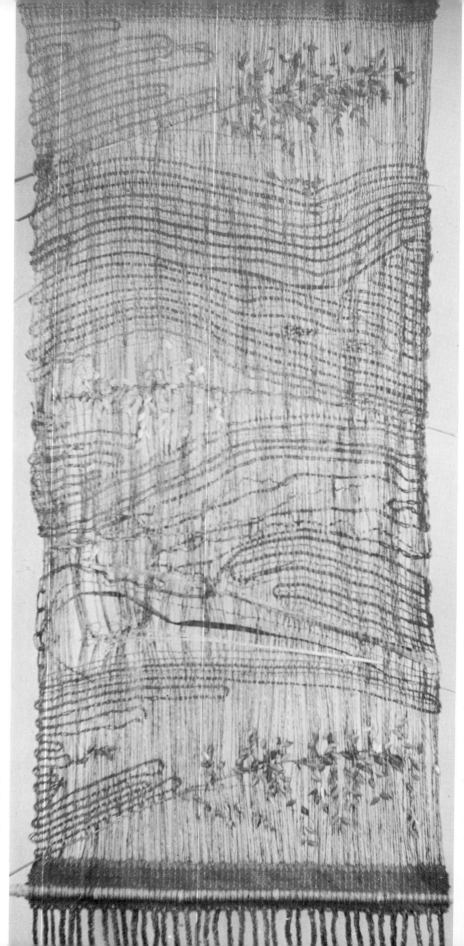

96

Fig. 56 Wall hanging
with weeds, by Helen
Henderson, U.S.A.
Warp and weft are
linen.

Fig. 57 Wall hanging (detail of upper part), by Helen Henderson.

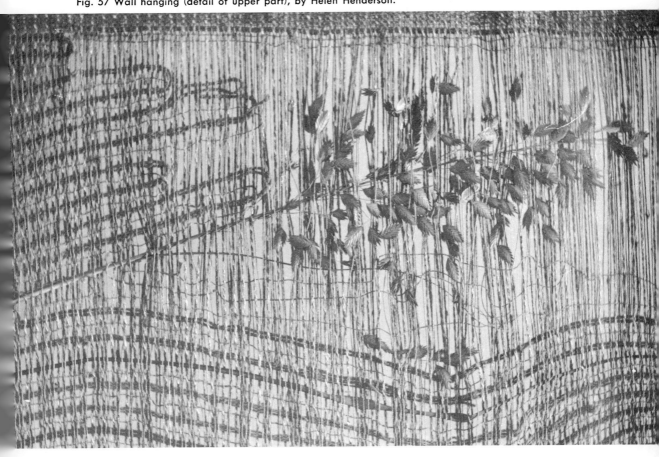

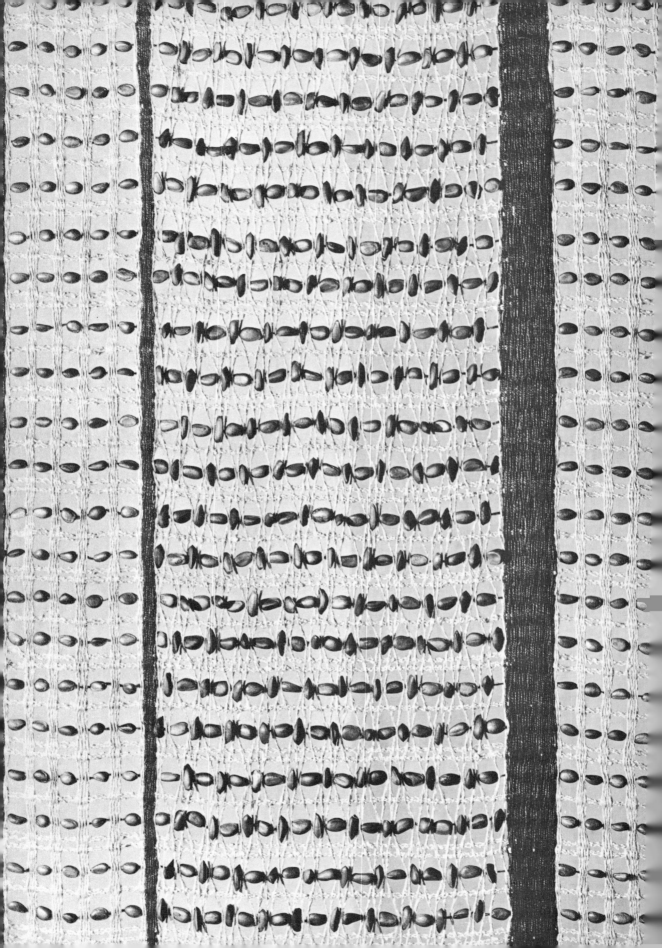

Opposite:
Fig. 58 Cherimoya seed panel, by Evelyn Gulick, U.S.A. Warp in linen, weft in linen bouclé and seeds; walnut slats are at the ends. *Photo by Harry Crosby.*

Fig. 59 Detail of cherimoya seed panel, by Evelyn Gulick. Seeds are strung on weft yarn (see left side). *Photo by Harry Crosby.*

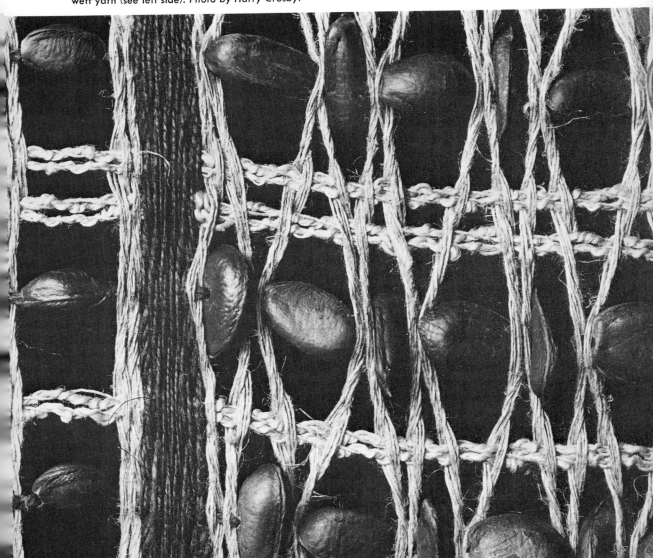

Chapter 7

Loom Preparation and Weaving Procedures

MAKING THE STRETCHER FRAME LOOM

Here is a visual presentation of how to construct a simple loom and set up the warp yarns ready to begin basic weaving procedures.

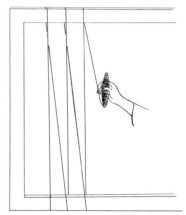

Fig. 60 Step 1: Take a spool with sufficient yarn on it. Tie the beginning on the lower left part of the frame in a knot, then guide the yarn over and under the top part of the frame. Now take the yarn to the lower frame, again over and under. Continue this procedure until all the warp yarns are on the frame.

Fig. 60 Step 1

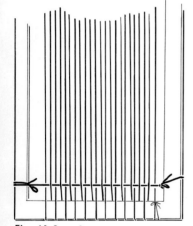

Fig. 61 Step 2: When all warp yarns are on the frame, put a ruler between top and bottom yarn layers and slide it downward; replace ruler with a long piece of string, and fasten it on either end, around the uprights.

Fig. 61 Step 2

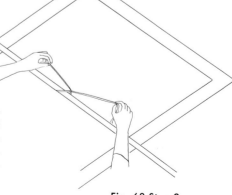

Fig. 62 Step 3: After you have guided, in over-and-under fashion, the second horizontal thread on the opposite side of the frame, place a ruler in the middle, on top of the frame. With a short string for the first heddle, go over and around the ruler, fasten on the edge, and let the two long ends of string needed for the next step hang.

Fig. 62 Step 3

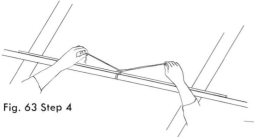

Fig. 63 Step 4

Fig. 63 Step 4: Take a long dowel stick and place it parallel to the ruler; guide the long string ends around the dowel stick, and make two secure knots. Cut the ends short.

Fig. 64 Step 5: After you have made two heddle rods as described, you start weaving. Wind the yarn over the long flat shuttle, raise the first heddle rod, and guide the shuttle through the two layers of shed.

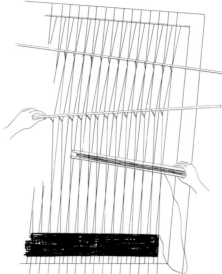

Fig. 64 Step 5

Fig. 65 Step 6: After the shuttle is guided out of the shed, put the yarn, or weft, in curves, zigzag fashion. This technique ensures that all the warp yarns will be covered. Then push the weft into the warp, downward toward the weaving, with a fork or other similar tool. Now raise the second heddle rod and continue in the same way.

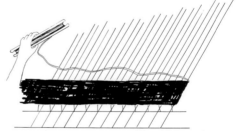

Fig. 65 Step 6

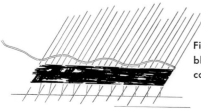

Fig. 66 Illustrating curving, or "bubbling," giving required weft yarn to cover all the warp.

BEFORE THE ARTIST WEAVES HIS project on the loom, he must be sure that he has sufficient material for both warp and weft. The weaver's yarns are made up in skeins, spools, or cones (Fig. 68), and are numbered in a precise and systematic way. He should know in advance just how many yards of thread each pound of material contains and how far the material will go.

WARP PREPARATION

Several steps, which do not necessarily have to follow any fixed order, must be taken before the weaving process gets under way. He must determine density—that is, the number of warp threads that will be required per inch. For an average warp hanging he may use about ten ends of threads. He must then determine the exact width of his projected tapestry or wall hanging.

The tapestry in our demonstration will be 40 inches wide, which means that the warp will require 400 threads, if there are to be 10 threads per inch throughout the entire fabric. After we know how many threads will be needed for the width of the tapestry, its length must be decided upon. If we plan to make the finished tapestry 3 yards long, we must add some extra length to allow for warp waste: The unwoven yarn ends tied to the rollers at the front and back of the loom. In addition to the unwoven warp, the length of unwoven material in the areas in front of the reed and in back of the harnesses must also be accurately ascertained. And since the warp will be in tension on the loom during the weaving process, we must allow for the shrinkage of the material that always occurs when it is removed from the loom. The size of the loom, the nature of the raw material, and

Fig. 67 Drawing of an Athenian vase, 500 B.C., representing scenes of weaving from raw material to finished textile. Two weavers are working on an upright warp-weighted loom at the right. Weaving starts at the top and continues downward. *The Metropolitan Museum of Art.*

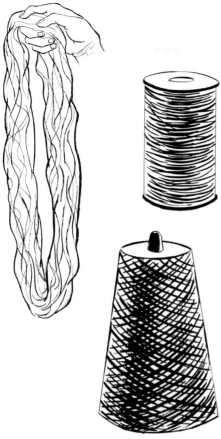

Fig. 68 Yarn in skein, cone, and spool, from left to right.

the nature of the weave construction are all factors that must be kept constantly in mind, for they determine how much warp must be added to the finished piece when the shrinkage has taken place. An average of one or two yards of unwoven warp is the customary allowance.

Before the weaver unwinds the spools of new yarns on the warping reel, he must again determine the number and length of the single threads that will be needed. In this case he must prepare 400 threads, each 5 yards in length. He then takes two spools and places them on the spool rack. Standing with the warping reel on his left and the spool rack on his right, he ties the two yarn ends from the spools to the first peg on the upper crossbar of the reel. With his right hand he then separates and arranges the threads over the pegs to form a warping cross. This keeps the

threads in consecutive order. The cross is formed between pegs 3 and 4, by alternating one thread at a time, over and under, between the two pegs (Fig. 69).

The weaver next revolves the reel and guides the threads around toward the right until the second crossbar and its two pegs are reached. The distance between the top and bottom pegs is the desired warp length—5 yards. Two threads are now on the reel, each 5 yards in length (Fig. 70).

From the bottom pegs, where the yarns have been guided together, over and under, the weaver carries them back up to the starting point while turning the reel in reverse. The first turn of two threads down across the board and the return of two back to the starting point provides four 5-yard warp threads, or the beginning of the warp. The back-and-forth guiding of the threads between the start-and-finish

pegs on the reel is continued until the necessary 400 lengths of warp yarn have been measured out.

When all of the required warp is on the reel, the crossing yarns are secured between the pegs on the top and bottom crossbars with a long piece of yarn of a different color from that of the warp. The weaver begins with the top cross of yarn on pegs 3 and 4, putting the tying yarn between the layers at peg 4. He then draws the tying, or security, thread through the other division, parallel with peg 3, and securely knots the ends of this thread. The bottom cross is then secured in the same way (Fig. 71).

When both crosses have been tied, the warp is ready to be taken from the reel. The weaver removes the warp from the top downward, winding it around his wrist to form the first loop, and chaining off the total threads, in hand-crocheting fashion (Fig. 72).

Fig. 69 The warping reel is on the table; at right is the spool rack. The weaver forms the warping cross between pegs 3 and 4.

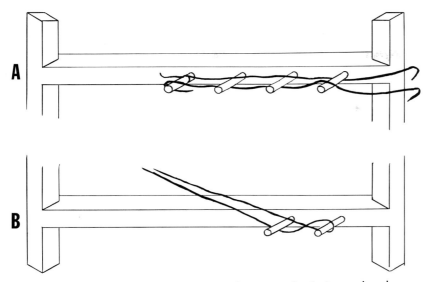

Fig. 70 Warping cross arrangements of yarns at beginning and end.
A. top cross, beginning. B. bottom cross, end of warp.

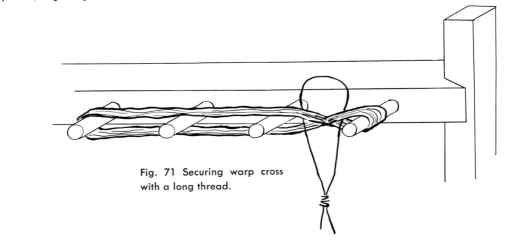

Fig. 71 Securing warp cross
with a long thread.

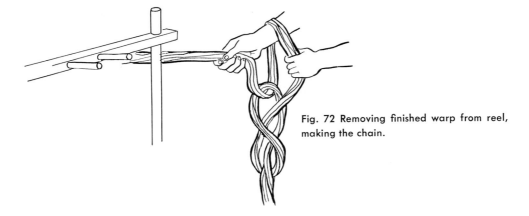

Fig. 72 Removing finished warp from reel,
making the chain.

PUTTING THE WARP ON THE LOOM

Beaming the warp, the next step, is accomplished by placing or winding the warp on the back roller attached to the loom. The finished warp, which is a chain of yarn, must then be evenly distributed along the roller beam to the width of the intended material. A tool called a "raddle" is used for this purpose (Fig. 73). It resembles a coarse comb, lidded on top. It is about as wide as the loom and has two dents, or openings, per inch.

The warp we are seeking here has 400 warp threads, consisting of 100 groups each, of the four yarns that were guided up and down from the two spools during the weaving process. It is at this point that the weaver, if all has gone well, begins to experience a feeling of accomplishment. Exacting challenges have been met and conquered, but much remains to be done. He must distribute the ends in the raddle comb to the planned, 40-inch width of the cloth, put five threads in each dent, and continue distributing the threads across the raddle in conformity with the complete width.

The task of putting the threads in the dents of the raddle can be accomplished on a table or on the loom. In our demonstration it is done with the raddle secured to the back beam above the warp roller. All the yarns are laid through the loom, directly over the shafts, with the ends projecting out over the front and back beams. The two-and-two grouped cross—the bottom cross —hangs over the raddle on the back beam. When the warp is in the loom, the weaver replaces the tying thread with a piece of string that is passed through the top section of the cross and tied to the ends of a stick that has been put through the lower section.

Yarn grouping into the raddle dents is done lightly, so that the long warp threads are not pulled, and stay securely in position. When thread distribution has been completed, a lid is placed on the raddle to prevent the grouped yarns from falling out of the dents while beaming. The stick to which the string that holds the warp is attached is now fastened by means of four or five extension cords to the roller.

Some of these procedures may seem complicated, but weaving is basically an easily mastered art, and once the initial steps have been taken there is a total absence of monotony.

To wind the wide warp on the beam perfectly, we must clear out as much as possible of the shafting and interference at the center of the loom. The winding is usually done by two individuals. One stands in front and the other at the back of the loom. The person in front holds the warp tightly while the other turns the warping beam (Fig. 74). The holder of the yarns must strive to give them tension. He must take great care not to allow them to be

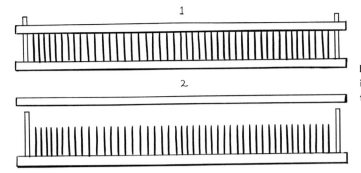

Fig. 73 1. raddle closed; 2. lid is removed, ready for yarn distribution.

Fig. 74 Warp winding. Person standing in front of loom holds the warp tight while the other winds the beam and also puts large sheets of brown paper into the warp.

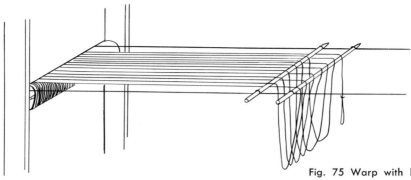

Fig. 75 Warp with lease sticks, drawn forward toward heddles.

pulled slackly through his hands. The person at the back turns the roller; and after some of the warp is on the loom, places between the warp layers of sheets of paper that prevent the quite soft yarns from forming grooves or acquiring uneven tension. For a 5-yard warp three sheets of brown wrapping paper, a little wider than the warp, are used. Winding is continued until the end or the warp reaches the beam above the warp roller.

The warp is then removed from the raddle, and the security thread on the top cross is exchanged for two sticks, which are inserted separately between the two divisions of the yarn. Since the yarns are on the roller, they can be safely spread out, and the complete warp, with lease sticks, can be drawn forward to the heddle frames. These brought-forward warp threads are cut near heddles and tied in bunches, preparatory to threading (Fig. 75).

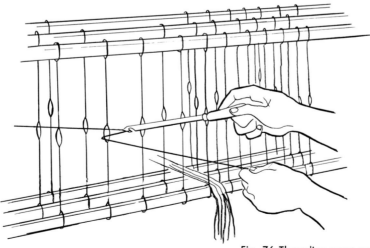

Fig. 76 Threading warp yarns through heddle eyes with the hook.

THREADING HEDDLES

One after another the threads are drawn through the heddle eyes with an entering hook—a long, flat crocheting needle (Fig. 76). The weaver draws the first warp thread by putting the hook through the first heddle eye on the first shaft. He then takes the second yarn and threads it through the first heddle on the second shaft. The third thread is put through the first heddle on the third shaft, and the next and final yarn through the first heddle eye of the fourth frame (Fig. 77). This completes the threading unit, which consists now of a straight draw threaded from front to back. We repeat the yarn threading until all the yarn ends on the loom are drawn through heddle eyes. After twenty or thirty have been threaded, they are tied for security.

When the entering process is complete, the warp ends are put through the dents in the reed. With a density of ten ends per inch, we use a ten-dench-per-inch reed. One yarn will be put through each dent, or opening. Before the yarns are guided through the dents, the warp is pulled toward the front, to ensure that the threads will be long enough for easy handling.

The entire procedure here is very similar to heddle threading. The hook is put through the dent, and the first yarn from shaft 1 is firmly grasped and pulled through the opening. The next thread is hooked through the next dent, and the threading process is continued until all the yarns are dented (Fig. 78). When the process is completed, the threads are group-tied, so that they hang from the reed securely.

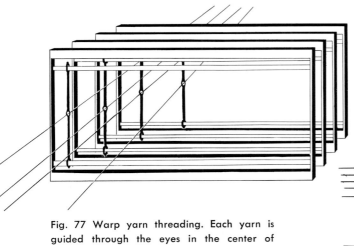

Fig. 77 Warp yarn threading. Each yarn is guided through the eyes in the center of heddles that are strung on the shafts.

Fig. 78 Entering, or venting, the warp yarns through the vents of the reed. This is usually done with the reed down, removed from the beater.

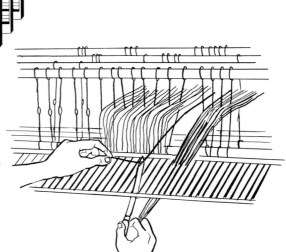

TYING THE WARP YARNS

The group-tied warp threads, dangling in bunches from the reed in front of the loom, must then be secured to the rod that is connected with the cloth roller by cords or by a sturdy fabric apron (Fig. 79). Before the weaver begins the warp tying, he guides rod and extension cords, or apron, around the roller and over the breastbeam.

In tying the yarns, the first small bunch on the left is divided into two parts and placed over and around the rod. It is fastened with a knot and a half-bow (Fig. 23). Next, the bunch on the right outer side is similarly divided, and then the center group. The remaining, or intervening, yarn groups are attached to the rods with the same kind of knots. The yarns are straightened before they are tied, so that the entire group will be in perfect alignment.

The weaver tests carefully for evenness and tension by going over the warp surface with his hand, and tightens the threads with the cloth roller ratchet. When he is satisfied that all the yarns are evenly tensioned, he arranges the shaft for the weave pattern.

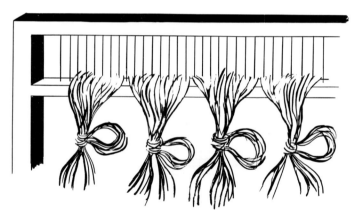

Fig. 79 Reed with hanging groups of tied warp.

SHAFT AND TREADLE TIE-UP

The shafts and lams are connected with the treadles on the floor. The lams are fastened to the shaft cords in sequence from front to back. A mending-type plain weave connects lams 1 and 3 with the first treadle, and lams 2 and 4 with the second. When the first treadle is pushed down, shafts 2 and 4 remain in an upright position, and when the second treadle is depressed, shafts 1 and 3 are raised. When this treadle-lam connection has been completed, the shuttles for yarns are prepared.

PREPARING THE SHUTTLES

For wall-hanging weaving various kinds of shuttles are chosen. For some projects the weaver prefers ordinary boat shuttles, and for others the flat kind. The yarn is wound from large spools onto smaller quills or bobbins by means of a winder. Quills are small paper tubes about 5 to 6 inches in length. These fit into a shuttle, and the yarn beginning is threaded through an eye located at the center of the boat. Flat shuttles are about 6 to 9 inches long and are made from wood or fiber.

If you are winding from a skein, place the skein around an adjustable winder. Cut the fastening strings and draw the beginning thread directly to the shuttle or other appropriate weft tool. There are two basic types of shuttles, the simple stick shuttle and the throw kind. The stick shuttle is made of a bar of wood or fiber from ⅛ to ¼ of an inch in thickness, with openings at the ends. These flat stick shuttles come in many lengths and widths. They are usually 1½ inches wide and 10, 14, 18, and 21 inches long.

Many weavers also use for wall-hanging weaving a rug shuttle that holds very thick yarns. It looks like two enlarged stick shuttles joined by crossbars. This shuttle usually measures 1 to 3 feet in length.

Tie the end of weft yarn with a slip knot to an end bar of the shuttle. Wind the thread around the end bars to fill the inside of the shuttle.

A throw shuttle is not so often used for tapestry weaving. However, if one weaves all across the width quite frequently, it is advisable to use one, since weaving is much faster. It is a boat-shaped device containing a bobbin for holding thread placed on a steel pin or heavy steel wire inserted in the shuttle opening. From the bobbin the thread comes through an opening at the front of the shuttle, and, as it is used, unreels gradually. Weaving with this throw shuttle is by far the quickest method, and is preferred by many weavers. The bobbin, or container, of the weft thread is called a cup or quill.

To wind these small quills it is necessary to use a bobbin winder. The tubelike cups are placed on the steel rod of the winder. This rod is tapered and is thickest at the end of the rod, near the turning device where it is fastened. Moving the quill toward the heavier end keeps it held tightly in place during the winding process.

A bobbin winder may be made by soldering a steel rod into the end of a rotating sander or some such device. The steel rod may also be attached to the bobbin winder of a sewing machine or may be inserted into an electric mixer, fan, or ordinary small motor.

Wooden bobbins are available

at weaving supply houses. However, bobbins can also be made at home out of wrapping paper. Cut the paper in half-moon shape with the straight edge of the half circle measuring an inch less than the length of the opening in the throw shuttle. Roll the half circle tightly around the rod of the bobbin winder, with the left side of the paper about ½ inch from the small end of the rod, and paste down the end of the paper on top.

To wind a bobbin, place it on the rod of the winder and move it toward the thicker end, so that it will be held firmly in place. Carry the thread to be wound upward from the spool. Bring its end up in back of the bobbin on the left side of the winder. Turn this short end down over the front of the bobbin, and wind the long end around it several times to hold it firmly in place.

Now start winding the bobbin by turning the handle of the bobbin winder clockwise.

In either a wooden bobbin or a homemade one the course of the thread should be guided gradually at first from left to right, but with backward and forward progression, similar to winding bobbins on a sewing machine. As the bobbin starts to fill, do not wind out the ends, but make it taper off on either end. Maintain a slight tension when winding, for the bobbin should be fairly firm and tight when finished.

Set the finished bobbin in the opening of the shuttle with the thread coming toward you from underneath. Thread the end through the hole on the rounded front side of the shuttle. Then insert the steel pin in place, passing it through the center of the bobbin and into the holes at the end of the wooden cavity. Shove it first into the end having the spring, and then adjust it into position at the other end.

Fig. 80 Half of the warp is raised, the other half down; the space between is called the "shed." The weaver throws the shuttle through the shed from left to right, back and forth.

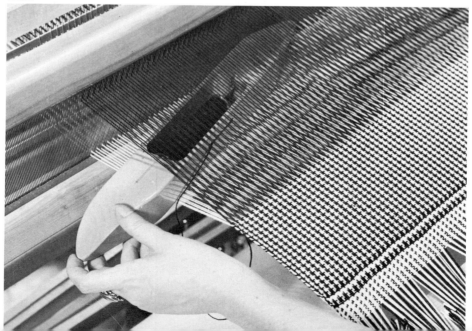

Fig. 81 The beater is pushed forward with the left hand, and the weft is pressed into the warp close to the last one.

WEAVING—INSERTING THE WEFT

A few definite, easy-to-master steps make up the operation known as weaving. First the treadle—dictated by the design—is pressed firmly down, creating the shed through which the shuttle is guided across the width of the material (Fig. 80). The weft is then pressed into the warp by moving the beater forward (Fig. 81). These three primary motions—warp opening, weft inserting, and beating—are comparatively simple ones, and no difficulty should be experienced in executing them. As soon as the woven cloth is near the beater, more warp has to be released from the warp roller. This replenishing motion is done at regular intervals, and soon becomes automatic. Beating varies with the desired density, and may be very firm, medium-firm, or light.

To weave with a throw shuttle, hold it in the left hand while the right hand pushes the beater back after having beaten down the last row. Give it a slight push by moving the wrist of the left hand, and send it through the opening to the other side. Then catch the shuttle with the right hand, while enough weft yarn unwinds. Leave the thread in either curved or slanting; bring the beater forward with the other hand, and then change the shed. Reverse the process, throwing with the right hand and catching with the left.

If you want a close weave, hold the beater toward or close to the weft; then change for the next opening, all the while holding the beater firmly.

OTHER LOOM PREPARATION METHODS

There are a number of other ways in which a loom can be set up and made ready for weaving. As in virtually all craft undertakings the individual artisan is free to choose the method that is most in accord with his personal preferences or the task he has set himself.

WARP METHOD OF ANCIENT WEAVERS

A small tapestry requiring a very short warp of 1 or 2 yards may be wound between two pegs projecting from the wall or board. The distance between the pegs, in this instance, would be 1 or 2 yards. The warp yarns are then guided around the pegs until you have the number required for the project. This, an ancient procedure, is still practiced a great deal.

The finished warp, secured with a yarn, is then transferred to the loom. Then you slip one end onto the warp roller and the other around the cloth, or front, roller. To form the warping cross, you guide a wide stick over and under the individual warp threads. Then, with another stick, the same procedure is made in reverse, starting under and over.

MAKING A WARP ON WARPING BOARD

Many weavers prefer a warping board that does not take up much space. This can be easily made. The warping board is a sturdy frame that consists of four bars of wood screwed together and braced at the four corners. These boards should be long enough to meet the weaver's requirements.

They are bored with holes into which the pegs are fitted. The distance between the pegs from left to right is a definite length, such as 1 yard, to aid the weaver in measuring the warp accurately. The pegs on the side bars are placed vertically from 5 to 7 inches apart, but the top one on the right is usually set about 2 inches higher than the top one on the left, so that the warp threads run diagonally downward each time across.

Across the top there are four pegs. The starting peg is placed 10 inches from the next peg on the upper bar. The distance between the second and third peg is 9 inches, and the last, or fourth, peg is placed 10 inches from the third one. The warping cross is made between the second and third cross, as shown in the illustration.

If you make this frame, first cut and sandpaper the side bars and bore holes for the pegs. Fasten the four bars together by inserting two bolts at each corner of the frame in the required position. Insert the pegs in the holes, place a wedge in a slit at the back of each peg, and then drive the pegs firmly into their holes.

Materials for this warping board are: four boards ¾ by 2½ by 42 inches, seventeen pegs, 1 inch by

6 inches, and eight bolts to fasten at each corner. Seventeen wedges will be needed to make the pegs fast, ⅛ of an inch thick, 1 inch wide, and 1½ inches long.

To make a warp on this frame place a spool with yarn in a basket beside the frame to keep it from rolling, and let the thread travel from the basket over a hook or through a screw eye over the warping board. Tie the end of the thread around the first upper peg on the left side, using a slice knot, and carry the thread over the next peg and under the third, over the fourth and the one on the far upper corner. Then guide the thread diagonally from side to side until the bottom peg is reached. Then reverse the direction until you come to the third peg of the upper crossbar. Here pass over where you previously went underneath, and under instead of over the next peg. Guide this thread down and upward until you have the required number of warp yarns on the frame.

In the warping process the tension of the individual threads is very important. If all of the threads are wound in the same tension, they will maintain similar lengths and will go on the warp roller easily and smoothly, without tangling. As different hands pull at different tensions, it is best for each weaver to finish his own warp.

When all the warping threads that have been made on this frame have been measured off, keep them together as a group by tying a short colored cord around them, as shown in the illustration. Slip the ends through the peg opening and tie the colored cord at the ends together in a single knot to make the warping cross. This keeps the threads in their proper order and prevents them from tangling.

To keep this cross proceed as follows: Before taking the warp from the frame, run the colored cord from the front through the opening of the second peg on the top bar, carry it around and out through the opening at the next, or third, peg, and then tie the ends as shown in the illustration. Also tie a short thread around the total warp at their reverse points.

To prevent the warp from becoming tangled, wind it in a chain as it is removed from the pegs. This process is known as "chaining off the warp."

Remove the warp at the lower peg, and loop the first part over your hand and pull a short continuous part through the formed loop. Continue this procedure, which resembles hand crocheting, until you reach the top cross, which should hang down. Now slip the long flat lease rods through the openings secured on the frame and fasten the long rods together with a cord or string at either end.

THREADING AND BEAMING THE WARP

The complete warp with the lease rods is now put on top of the loom's front beam, with the ends of the rod toward the reeds. Cut the tying cords and spread out the threads. Then cut through the ends of the loops, making single ends of thread. Our next task is to thread the warp, this time from the front of the loom to the back.

The reed, a comblike tool with steel dents spaced at even distances, is in the loom's beater, which is now in front of the hanging warp threads. Start threading the yarns at one side, and put the first pair of warp threads as they come from the lease rods through the first required dent, just at the beginning of the needed width for weaving. Then put the second pair of warp threads through the next dent. This provides for double warp threads at both sides, making a stronger selvage. Now pass a single thread through each dent in succession until you come to the last two dents. Here again, thread a pair of warp threads through to make this side identical with the other first side.

After all the warp threads have been threaded through the dents of the reed, their ends lie in back of the reed but in front of the heddles of the harnesses. The next step is to thread them through the eyes of the heddles in the proper order. Take each thread in succession through the eyes on alternate harnesses. Put the first thread through your first heddle eye, the second through the heddle eye on the second shaft, and continue in the same way through the eyes of shafts 3 and 4. The crochet-like threading

hook may be used for drawing the warp threads through the eyes or loops of the heddles.

The next step is to attach the warp threads to the warp roller at the back of the loom, so that they can be wound around this for future use. Pull the threads through from the back of the harnesses toward the back beam on the loom. Tie these hanging threads in groups to the rod connected to the beam. Take about twenty warp threads, divide them into equal parts, and guide them over and around the rod, making on top a knot and a half-bow. The remaining warp threads are then tied in the same fashion.

Now from the front of the loom run the warp through your fingers or coarse comb until any tangles in the first two feet have been pulled through the warp and toward you. Then start turning the warp roller until all the knots around the rod are facing you on top of this beam. Slide on top of them a sheet of brown wrapping paper not too long and a little wider than your needed tapestry width. Continue turning the beam until two feet of warp are left in front of the reed. Beaming the warp or winding on the roller is often done by two weavers, one holding the warp in front of the loom while the other is turning and watching the warp beam in the back.

This beaming process is not difficult. Hold the warp with both hands, pulling it very taut while your partner winds up all the warp that remains untangled on the warp roller. When new tangles reach the reed, step out in front of the loom another three feet, divide the warp between your hands and proceed as before. In winding, always hold the warp tight, with all of the threads at the same tension. After a few rounds on the roller the new warp has a tendency to cut down into former rounds, thus shortening some of the threads and causing lumps across the width of the warp, or a curved warp with an unevenly filled beam may be formed. Therefore additional sheets of paper must be inserted whenever necessary.

When a wall hanging is woven on a low loom, both the preparation and the actual weaving process closely parallel that of ordinary yardage weaving. But the procedure becomes much more specialized when there are traditional, tapestry-weaving techniques that must be adhered to, or the weaver has some ambitious design in mind.

WARPING THE VERTICAL TAPESTRY LOOM

The modern upright tapestry loom equipped with roller beams is warped in the same manner as the ordinary hand loom, but may differ markedly in several ways. For instance, over and under or figure-eight method is used for warping the simple tapestry frame. It makes a warp that cannot be moved or rolled into a beam, so that the length of the weaving is determined by the distance of the heddle bar from the front stretcher, after allowance has been made for warp flattening and shed making.

On the larger upright, frame-type floor loom, the warp is also done right on the loom. If there is no reed, warp spacing is accomplished by chaining or twining a cord across a warp.

The following procedure should be followed in twining: First cut a strong cord about four times the loom width and stitch the center to the sidepiece near the front stretcher. Then knot this pair of cords near the first warp end, and take one under the first warp to the top. Carry the second over this and under the second warp. Take the first end over this second arrangement and under the third warp and continue with alternate ends, always carrying the end over the other twining cord and under the next warp. When the entire warp has been twined, tie the cords into a knot at the position of the last warp and fasten them around the stretcher, making sure that both of the two knots have been securely tightened.

A twined warp should also have a warp cross formed by two lease sticks. If there is no cross, one can be made by picking up alternating warps and inserting a stick in the shed thus formed. All the warps lying under this stick are then lifted, and a new stick is inserted in the second shed. The rear lease stick, which forms the fundamental shed, is then pushed to the back of the loom, and the front stick is placed midway between heddle rod and front stretcher.

The next step is a quite simple one. A heddle-tying guide is made by laying the wider shed stick on the warp in front of the heddle-bar holders, and tying it firmly to the sidepieces. The diagonal distance from the bottom of the heddle bar to the warp threads in front of this stick should be a little greater than the vertical distance from the heddle bar to the warps lying under the fundamental shed stick.

Mark on the heddle bar the positions the first and last heddles should occupy. Now roll the warp twine into a very tight ball and tie the beginning of this cord to the bar a little to the right of the right-hand position and encircle it with half hitches until the heddle bar is reached. Now we are in a position to proceed as follows with the making of the heddles: Carry the cord around the first warp thread that lies on the lease stick and pull it against the guide bar. Then carry the cord over the top and around the heddle bar at the left. Guide the cord around the bar at the right of the heddle and make a half hitch, then to the left and around the bar, and half hitch again.

We must then push the cords to the right, so that they will be closely spaced, before pulling them together to tighten the knots. When this is done we must make two more half hitches around the bar to the left. The same procedure is repeated with each heddle, and although this traditional form of heddle tying may seem a little awkward at first, it is greatly favored by many weavers.

Fig. 82 With the left hand the weaver pushes down the heddles needed for making the shed and inserting a bobbin with weft. *Photo by Jan Yoors.*

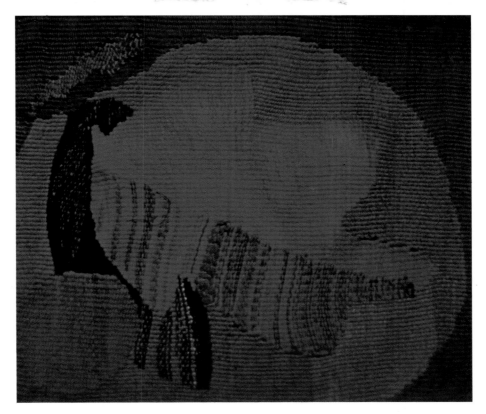

AUTUMN by Lili Blumenau. *Photo by Ferdinand Boesch.*

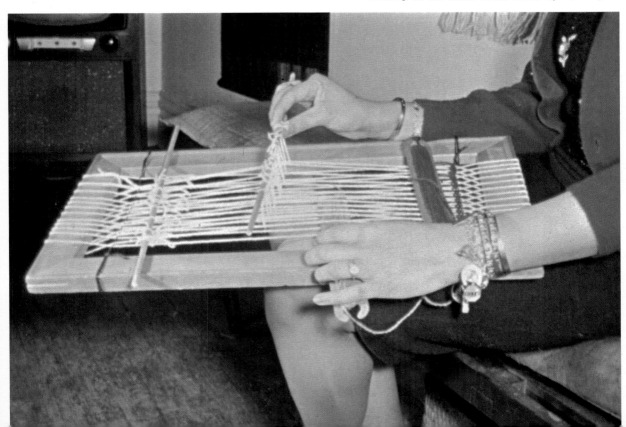

A. TRANSPARENT AND OPAQUE by Lili Blumenau. Fine rayon and novelty yarn and braided ribbon.

B. FLOATING LEAVES by Lili Blumenau. Heavy linen, wool, and handspun Haitian cotton.

C. COUNTRY by Lili Blumenau. Wool, cotton, and rayon.

D. HOMAGE TO PERU, a Lili Blumenau design. Lace weaves on solid tapestry rib background in all wool.

All photos by Len Depas.

A.

B.

C.

D.

Fig. 83 With the right hand a short weft is pushed down by means of a pointed tool. *Photo by Jan Yoors.*

WEAVING ON UPRIGHT VERTICAL LOOM

If this tapestry loom has harnesses, as on the horizontal warp loom, sheds are made in the usual way. If the loom has the shed stick and string heddles with a movable heddle bar, the shed is made by lifting the heddle bar from the lower to the upper position. In the usual arrangement with fixed heddle bar, the heddle shed is made by pulling a group of heddles downward and outward (Fig. 82). In making the shed, the fingers of the left hand are placed under the top warp threads, high in the shed. They bring forward the warp threads that are to be woven. To make a shed, the fingers work in both the heddles and the shed. The bobbin is always held in the right hand, whether working to the left or right side. The weft is inserted in the shed under only a few inches of warp, according to the requirements of the pattern.

The bobbin is then taken out, leaving the weft in a loose arc; this is called "bubbling the weft." It is then pushed downward with the end of the bobbin or other similar instrument (Fig. 83). Every few inches the weaver traces the design on the warp yarns (Figs. 83a, 83b). When finished, and enough lines are seen, weaving continues. This procedure continues until the tapestry is finished.

Fig. 83a The design is traced on the warp with a black inked brush or marker. Part of the whole cartoon is behind the warp for correctness of tracing. *Photo by Jan Yoors.*

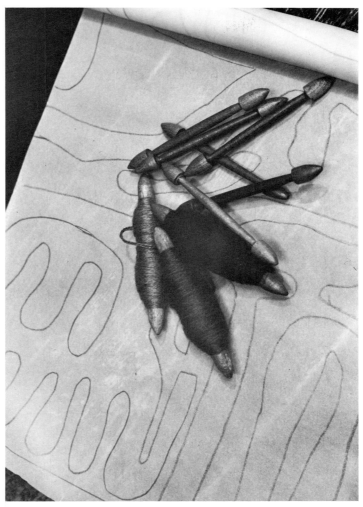

Fig. 83b A tracing is placed behind the warp so the weaver can paint the pattern on the warp yarns. Bobbins with weft yarn are displayed on the tracing. *Photo by Jan Yoors.*

FINISHING THE WALL HANGING

After the wall hanging has been cut from the loom, considerable freedom of choice is given for the finishing. Some artists make a wide hem at either side, weaving on top and bottom four or five inches in close weaving. Another way is to have a hem on top and fasten a stick behind for hanging on the wall; on the bottom are long warp fringes. Very often a flat stick is inserted in the warp before beginning the wall hanging. The same is done on the top part. After the stick has been put into the warp, several inches in plain weave are made across the entire width, and then hemmed underneath.

Chapter 8
Weave Techniques and Methods

THE WEAVE IS SIMPLY THE IN-
terlacing that takes place
between the warp and the
weft. The term is sometimes used
more broadly—and often errone-
ously—but that need not concern us
here. Wall hangings are executed
by various methods, and there are
many different kinds of weaves and
manipulative procedures.

Functional considerations play
an important role in the choice of a
weaving method. But the aesthetic
factor is of equal importance; and
when the choice is uncertain and
hangs in the balance, the weaver's
individual preferences may tip the
scales in favor of the simplest of
two or more methods.

In the choice of the weave itself,
the determining factor is often more
complex. An almost photographic
representation, for instance, needs
specific tapestry weave knowledge
and selective skill, and if one feels
like making a fantastic landscape
the best choice for interpretive
purposes is simple plain weave,
loose or closely woven.

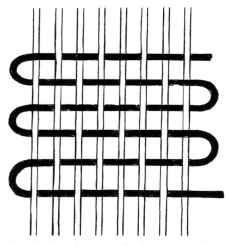

Fig. 84 Line drawing of plain weave. From
top to bottom are lengthwise warp yarns, and
heavy horizontal blacks are the weft thread,
interlacing over and under the warp.

PLAIN WEAVE

Plain weave is the basic warp-and-
weft interlacing (Fig. 84). It
closely resembles mending. In this
weave a single warp thread passes
over one weft and under the next,
and the same procedure is repeated
throughout the cloth. It is used in
the majority or interpretations (Fig.
84a).

122

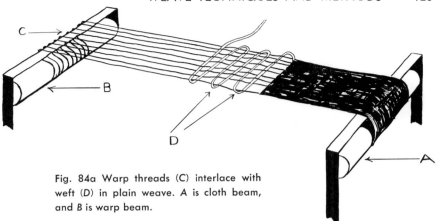

Fig. 84a Warp threads (C) interlace with
weft (D) in plain weave. A is cloth beam,
and B is warp beam.

There are many varieties of interlacing in addition to plain weave, and each one has a distinctive character. Some of them are simply enlarged or modified plain weave; others are less fundamental in character. There are satin weaves, basket weaves, twills arranged in many created patterns, and weaves so highly specialized that they are seldom used in wall hangings.

Plain weave is especially effective in tight constructions, but so numerous and varied are its uses that only some of them can be described here. A common construction is as follows: Compose bands of warp yarns with open or closed areas. Weave the traditional Spanish lace—three wefts of plain weave —across one warp band, beat with a fork, and guide the weft thread down to the next band. Then weave three rows of plain weave, and continue this manipulation all across the cloth until the design is completed. Or weave plain construction across each warp band, tight or open, and after some inches secure the ends and use plain weave across

the width of the hanging. Each of these weft yarns can also be long, and go on top of the plain-weave area after it has been woven.

An equally interesting construction is useful in achieving texture and breaking up solidly woven areas. Space warp threads quite far apart, so that wefts cover them. Weave one row of light threads alternating with dark, achieving uprights. With two wefts of light and dark alternating, you get another surface, and experimentation can then be made to yield variations of extreme diversity.

In using plain weave to shape fantastic landscapes, you may arrange the weft threads in any position you wish—to form circles, flowering plants, or wandering lines. Raise alternating warp threads, shape weft thread, and close warp; then continue by raising the opposite warp yarns for further arrangements. The procedure is a simple one, but holding the composition in place requires considerable skill. Your tools are necessarily the fingers and a fork.

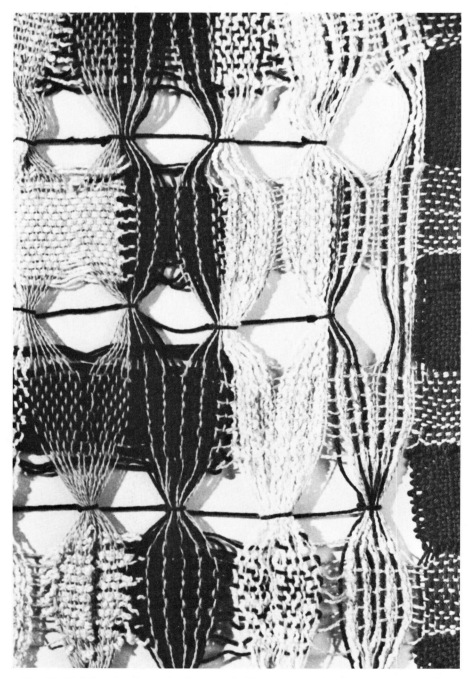

Fig. 85 Wall hanging has striped warp of different yarns. Bands are woven in plain weave across, alternating with open spaces created by bunching yarn groups with one weft. By a student in the Lili Blumenau weaving workshop. *Photo by Rudy Bleston.*

Fig. 86 Wall hanging in plain weave. After each woven stripe, some warp threads are crossed and tied with short yarn. By a student in the Lili Blumenau weaving workshop.

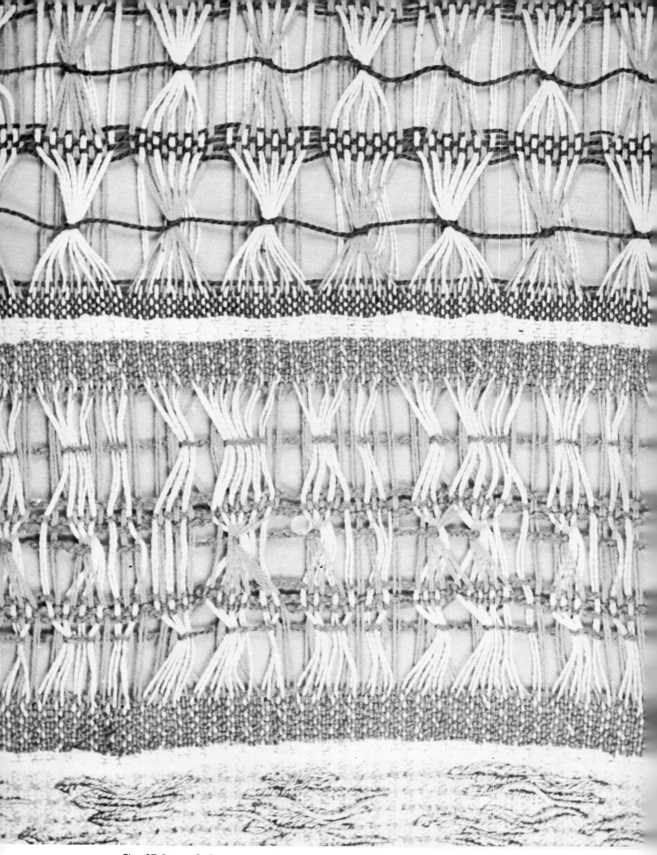

Fig. 87 Rows of plain weave alternating with groups of tied warp. By a student in the Lili Blumenau weaving workshop.

Fig. 88 WINDOWS, a wall hanging by Else Regensteiner, U.S.A. The frame is in plain weave. In the center, groups of warp yarns are closely tied together.

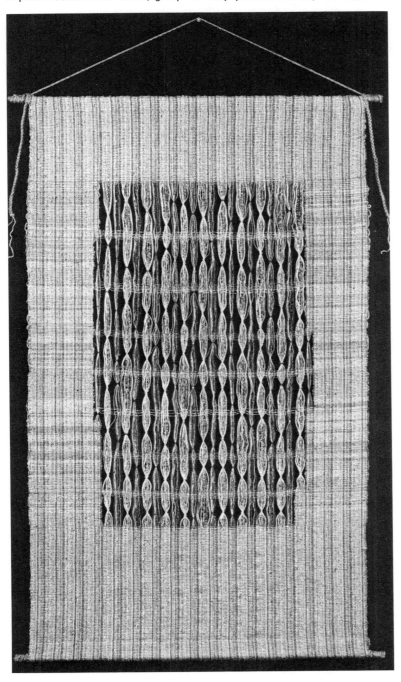

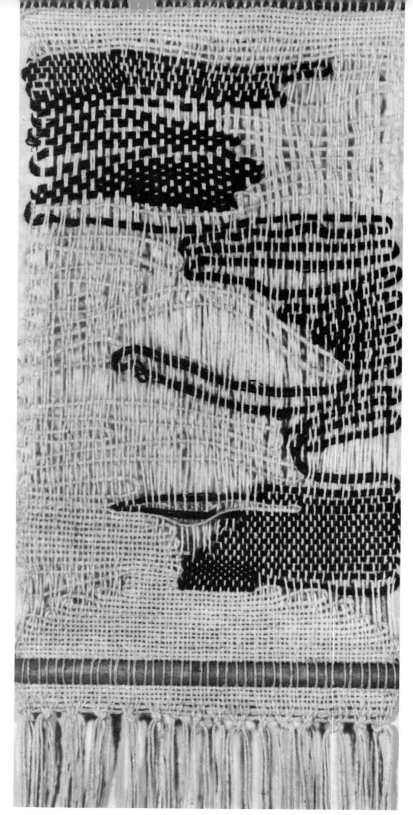

Fig. 89 SEA AND LAND, by Spencer Depas, Haiti. Weft interlaced loosely in plain weave and shaped with a fork to create the motif.

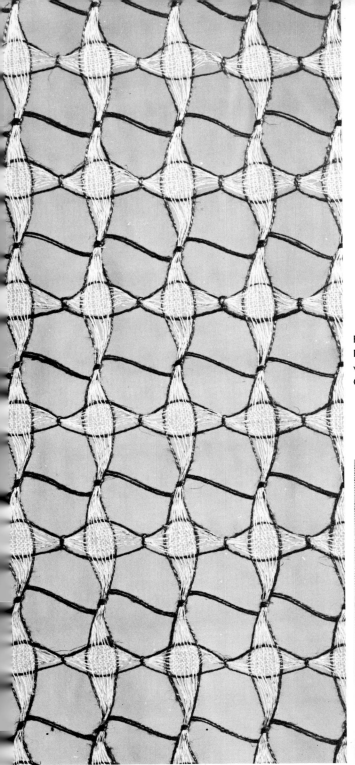

Fig. 90 BROWN TRACERY (detail), by Evelyn Gulick, U.S.A. Plain weave and weft tying to form stars. *Photo by Harry Crosby.*

Fig. 91 ST. MICHAEL AND THE DRAGON, by Martta Tiapale, Finland. Plain weave is used for the tapestry. Here the warp shows in equal distance as weft.

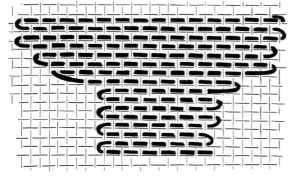

Fig. 92 Diagram showing laid-in technique.

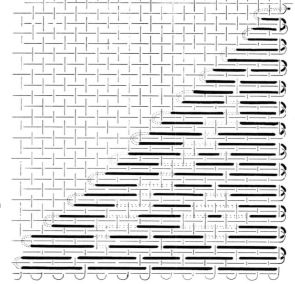

Fig. 93 Diagram of brocaded thread in black; background is plain weave.

LAID-IN METHOD

An interesting project for the weaver is the fashioning of designs, squares, or people on a plain-weave background. This is called "laid-in" weaving. For the background weave plain all across the material, and for the needed design—a square, for instance—lay in another colored thread on top of the background plain-weave row. Continue to weave across the material horizontally, and use a colored weft for the square. You may vary the weave for the ornament. This is usually done with a stick. The desired warps are lifted to permit the pattern thread to be laid in.

Laid-in weaving can be both varied and highly original. The background can be transparent and the motifs closely woven (Fig. 92). Or, in a more intricate construction, a large variety of yarns can be used, and the motifs combined according to the judgment and taste of the weaver.

Brocading is a technique frequently used in wall hangings. A brocade consists of an added design thread on a foundation of plain or other weaves (Fig. 93). It is similar to embroidery, and sometimes, as in not a few ancient Peruvian textiles, it is difficult to tell whether the fabric is woven or embroidered. Brocades are done either in small sections or from selvage to selvage. The long stitches are either horizontal (weft brocade) or vertical (warp brocade).

The background construction need not be in plain weave, but most brocade weavers prefer the more elementary varieties of interlacing.

To make the subject or ornament, pick up the needed warp and insert another colored weft. Then weave the background, return the colored weft to the fabric and complete the ornament. The background can be a fancy twill, or herringbone zigzag and brocading for the design still another interlacing. There are many stimulating ideas which will come to you if you make a careful study of ancient brocades from all over the world.

The real or traditional tapestry construction consists of the rib weave, which is derived from ordinary plain weave. In plain weave the same spacing or warp and weft is used, but in rib tapestry there are fewer warp threads and more than twice as many wefts. The use of this weave is not entirely confined to traditional tapestry.

A tapestry is composed of many independent color areas and joining these requires specific methods. To weave colored wefts all across the material presents no difficulties, for it is a quite simple procedure. But tapestry joinings are more complex. Many other methods are used, but the ones which we have described here are the most essential.

Fig. 94 YEN, by Mildred Fischer, U.S.A. Wall hanging in laid-in technique. Motifs are closely woven with thick weft; the background is transparent. *Photo by Jack Foster.*

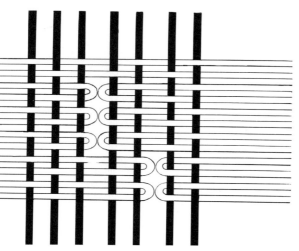

Fig. 95 Diagram showing slit technique. Interlacing between warp
and weft is in plain weave.

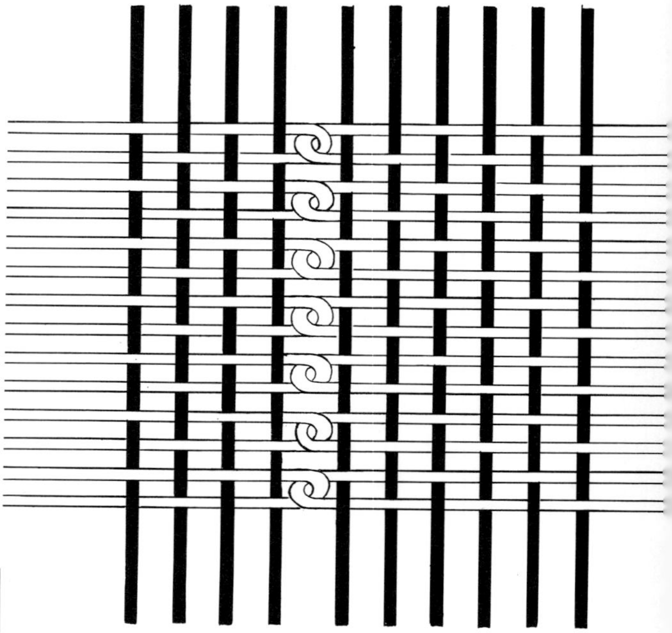

Fig. 96 Interlocking technique. Interlocking the wefts makes stronger
boundaries than slit technique.

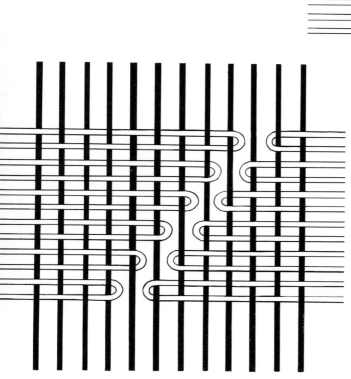

Fig. 97 Diagonal slit technique, used
to make diagonal outlines of a
motif.

TAPESTRY TECHNIQUES

Slit or Kilim

Either is the technical name for the slits that are left between the different colored areas. Each colored weft is woven back and forth across the length of an area, as if it were an independent cloth. This leaves slits, or openings, between the adjacent areas that may be sewn together afterwards (Fig. 95).

Interlocking

In this method the adjacent wefts are interlocked with each other between the boundary warp threads. In interlocking after each woven weft, great care must be taken to use the same direction in the same shed. When weaving pairs, every alternate can be interlocked. This method is both simpler and faster (Fig. 96).

Diagonals

A diagonal joining needs no locks, as the gradual moving secures the margin. A diagonal is right-angled or steep in accordance with the number of wefts that are made before the line is moved. To make the line steeper we must use more wefts. This procedure is similar to the slit method. Many shapes can be developed in this joining process, but the margins must be moved with painstaking care (Fig. 97).

Fig. 98 Surface effects for motifs in tapestries. The warp is completely covered. Stripe is solid color. Stripe 2 is three light wefts and one dark, alternating. Stripe 3 is three dark wefts and one in light, alternating. Stripe 4 is two dark wefts alternating with two in light yarn.

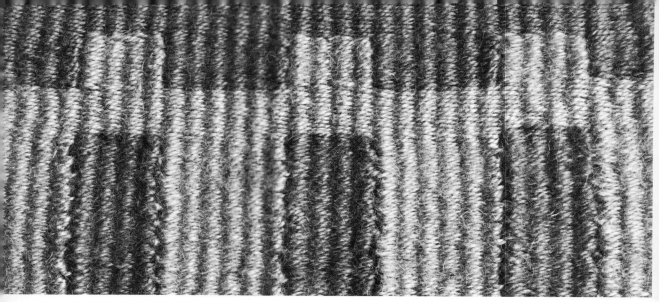

Fig. 99 Detail of a tapestry with geometrics, by Lili Blumenau. Slit and interlocking techniques are combined.

When the weaving areas are bound by diagonals, it is possible to build up one color area for the full distance of the weft before work is started on the adjacent area. Most of the large French tapestries are woven in this manner.

Although the traditional tapestry-joining techniques are everywhere the same, methods differ greatly. The artist who re-creates the painting or cartoon from which the tapestry is woven usually requires weavers as highly skilled as the Aubusson or Gobelins craftsmen.

Many of these weavers have become specialists in weaving by dint of long experience in the highly specialized field of detailed cartoon geometrics and reproductions of foliage. Tapestry weaving of this kind requires the strictest kind of self-discipline and absolute techniques. These world-famous hangings can be reproduced over and over, since the artist-designer makes the cartoon, and weaving is done by skilled craftsmen.

The contemporary artist-weaver concept is more flexible, and there is a much closer union between the expressive idea and its execution. The artist-weaver is more concerned with the artistic quality of the work than with perfected and virtually flawless weaving skill, although he strives never to neglect the latter factor. He combines a variety of weaving methods, changes densities more often, and uses a wider variety of yarns to achieve expressive surfaces. The overall impression conveyed by the finished tapestry is one of greater strength. The artist-woven tapestry is unique and cannot be created in fragmentary fashion, no matter how much technical skill is used to compensate for the loss of creative inspiration and unity that the dividing up of the work makes inevitable.

Fig. 100 Detail of a tapestry in diagonal method, by Lili Blumenau.

Opposite:

Fig. 101 Tapestry by Esther Gotthofer, U.S.A. The tapestry is woven sideways on the loom.

Fig. 102 SLY FOX (detail) tapestry by Ines Tuschnerova, Czechoslovakia. The moving margins of the shapes are in slit-tapestry technique.

Fig. 103 LA FILLE AUX MOUETTES (detail), tapestry by Mary Dambiermont, Belgium. The artist uses fine yarns and elaborate shapes.

Fig. 104 GEOMETRICAL MOTIFS, tapestry by Esther Gotthofer.

Fig. 105 L'ASTRE NOIR, an elaborate abstraction by Maurice André, France. *Photo by Annet Held.*

Fig. 106 CÔTE D'OR, tapestry designed by Michel Tourlière, France, and woven in Aubusson at the Fabrique de Tapisseries Suzanne Goubely-Gatien.

Fig. 107 THE CONSTELLATION OF TAURUS, by Hana Lendrova, Czechoslovakia. The tapestry was woven sideways on the loom.

Fig. 108 DANSEUSE AU JARDIN (detail), tapestry by Antonin and Ludmiler Kybal, Czechoslovakia. *Photo by Karla Neuberta.*

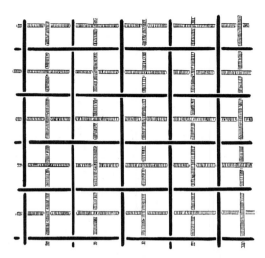

Fig. 109 Yarn interlacing for tubes of double cloth in plain weave. Black lines show top layer, shaded lines, back layer.

DOUBLE CLOTH

The double-cloth weave and method contribute greatly to the originality of wall hangings, in the hands of a gifted artist-weaver. It is a very ancient method indeed, and was used quite extensively in Peru and medieval Europe. We have many shining examples of this weave, and even the more classical ones will suggest new ideas and widen the scope of improvisation for the contemporary craftsman.

Double cloth consists of two fabrics, a top and bottom layer, woven alternately or separately, but on one warp (Fig. 109). This double textile is often stitched together at intervals. When double cloth is made without stitching the face and back together, a tubular material results. Top and bottom layers are woven or stitched together along the selvage, and both layers can be done in a variety of weaves. In wall hangings the top and bottom are usually in plain-weave construction.

To weave simple plain double cloth raise the warp thread, leave threads 2, 3, and 4 down, and continue in this manner all across the warp. Then enter the weft. For the next row, raise thread 3, leave the three adjacent threads down, and weave a row. This makes a top layer in plain weave. For the bottom row of plain weave raise the first three warp yarns, leave the next down, and repeat across the construction before laying in the weft. To make the next alternating pattern lift thread 1, keep the next down, and lift 3 and 4; then continue the same rotation across the construction until the weft is reached and entered.

The variations that can be made in this construction are numerous. Weave 2 inches of plain weave for the bottom layer, and leave the remaining warp threads loose or uneven on top of the cloth. Then tie, twist, or decorate in any way you desire. Tying is simple. Just wind a thread around some of the unwoven warp threads, and when they are secured repeat the procedure all across the construction.

In double weave twisting is done in various leno techniques, either manually or with a pickup stick. You may also combine leno twisting with areas in top-layer plain weave, as in the accompanying illustrations (Figs. 116, 117, 118). Loose-hanging warp yarns from a double-cloth layer may also be shaped into motifs that are extremely expressive and appealing. Or make a composition of horizontal bands of alternating lengths of 2 and 4 inches; unite the top and bottom layers in plain weave and start a differently proportioned band. Divide the bands on your composition as you proceed into rectangles or brickwork squares. For each band area select a distinctive technique. You may choose, for instance, plain weave loose or tightly woven, novel ways of twisting or tying, or shaping geometrics that provide the scope that is needed for highly imaginative experimentation.

A more elaborate double-cloth technique that is ideally suited to the weaving of wall hanging abstractions, with their sharp tonal contrasts, is the reversible "Finnweave." Select a dark color for threads 1 and 2, and a light one for 3 and 4, and weave as follows: Start on left selvage, with the first thread dark, and threads 3 and 4 light, and make the bottom dark halfway. Raise dark 2 with light 3 and 4 and weave with dark second for bottom layer. Raise light 3 and weave with light thread and raise next light 4 to return. To make the right dark area, lift threads 1, 2, and 4 together and weave with light thread; then raise 1, 2, and 3 for the next light weft. For the dark top layer raise thread 1, weave with dark, and raise yarn 2, returning to dark. By this same method the unusual black-and-white reversible construction that has just been described can be elaborated upon in various ways, with or without decorations, according to the taste and individual preferences of the weaver. Rectangles in contrasting colors, spirals, and whorls are but a few of the abstract patterns that can add beauty to the textural effects that can be achieved by the artist-designer who has experimented freely with reversible "Finnweave."

Fig. 111 GALAXY II, tapestry in modified double weave, by Glen Kaufman, U.S.A.

Fig. 110 KORPPA, tapestry in double weave, by Maija-Liisa Forss-Heinonen, designer; Helmi Vuorelma, weaver, Finland.

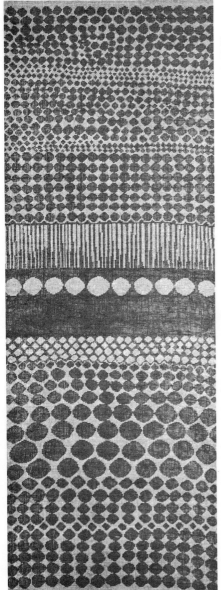

Fig. 112 PIMPULA PAMPULA, tapestry in double cloth, by Maija-Liisa Forss-Heinonen, designer; Helmi Vuorelma, weaver, Finland.

Fig. 113 NETS, by Kay Sekimachi, U.S.A. "Finn-weave,' or double-weave, tapestry.

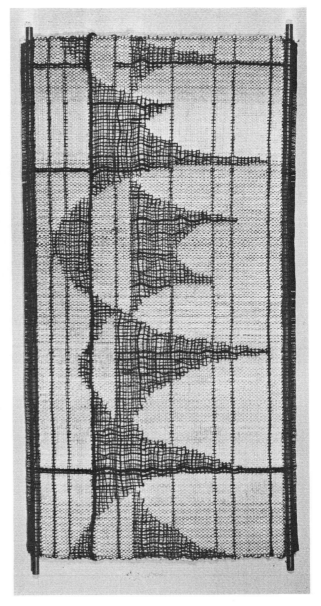

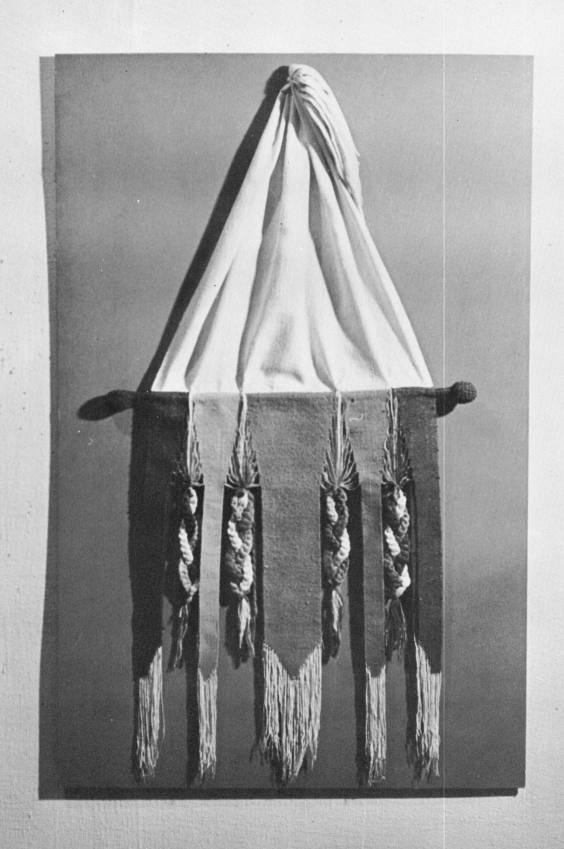

Opposite:
Fig. 114 CARNIVAL, by Claire Zeisler, U.S.A. Woven form in double weave.
Fringes are crocheted.

Fig. 115 CARNIVAL (detail), by Claire Zeisler. See band on left side; it is on
top of another one.

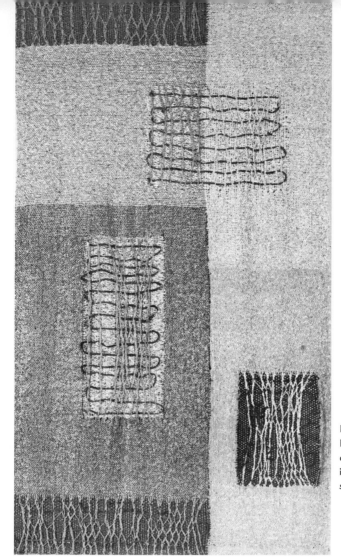

Fig. 116 Wall hanging, by Lili Blumenau, U.S.A., in double cloth and fancy leno. Warp yarn is rayon bouclé; weft for leno is *soutache* (Russian braid).

Fig. 117 Wall hanging with fancy leno (detail), by Lili Bulmenau.

Fig. 118 Wall hanging, by Spencer Depas, Haiti, with leno decoration. Wool is warp and weft. There are greater facilities to shape the weft in double cloth leno.

Fig. 119 Detail of leno section by Spencer Depas, Haiti, clearly shows the weft shaping.

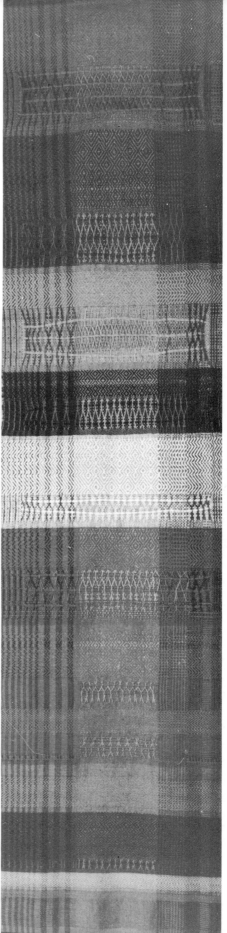

149

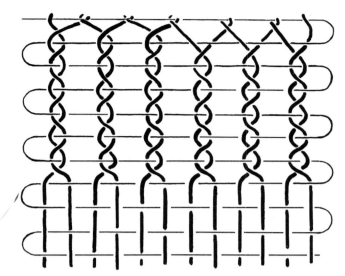

Fig. 120 Diagram shows four wefts in plain weave, with the remainder in single leno twist.

LENO OR GAUZE WEAVE

Open or transparent hangings are very much in vogue today, and the leno style, or lace weave, is just right for this technique. Plain leno is also called gauze, and is commercially known as marquisette. The weave is frequently used in lace curtains or casements. Here the warp yarns cross each other as they do in braiding. The constant twisting and turning enable the weaver to space the wefts a considerable distance apart, as they are held tight whenever reversing occurs.

The simplest way to make plain leno is on closed warp threads. Take a pickup stick or long knitting needle, start at right selvage and cross warp threads 2 and 1. Between the crossing insert the stick or needle. Then turn thread 4 over 3 in the same manner, and continue all across the construction. To insert the weft slant the pickup stick or replace it with a wider one. For the second row insert the stick under threads 2, 4, and 6 and continue across the construction toward the right selvage. This single-thread twisting can also be done more mechanically, but in wall hangings it is advisable to use the simplest hand-controlled method.

A considerable number of variations can be obtained here by alternating the threads quite freely (Figs. 120, 121, 122). The two-twist single threads, for instance, can be alternated with three threads in adjacent three warp yarns, with some rows of plain weave in between. With plain weave combined with leno the variations possible are almost limitless.

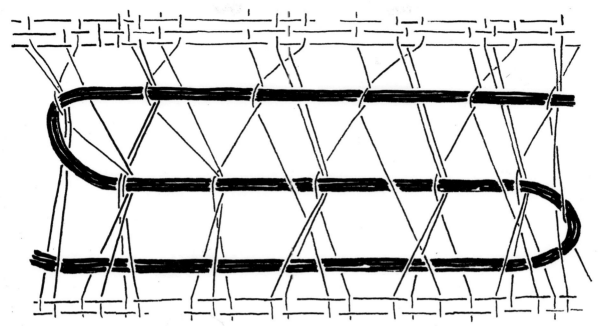

Fig. 121 Fancy leno twisting with several warp threads.

Fig. 122 Leno combined with plain weave. It is a so called Greek leno.

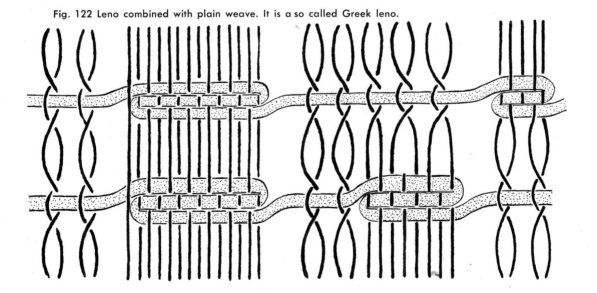

Fig. 123 CROSS AND SUN, wall hanging by Lili Blumenau, U.S.A.
Original leno technique with plain-weave shapes forming the design.
Photo by Ferdinand Boesch. Collection, Lili Blumenau.

Opposite:
Figs. 124 and 125 CROSS AND SUN (details), by Lili Blumenau.

Fig. 126 Wall hanging by Mrs. Brantley Henderson, U.S.A. Plain weave and gauze techniques.

Opposite:
Fig. 127 Wall hanging (detail showing upper part), by Mrs. Brantley Henderson.

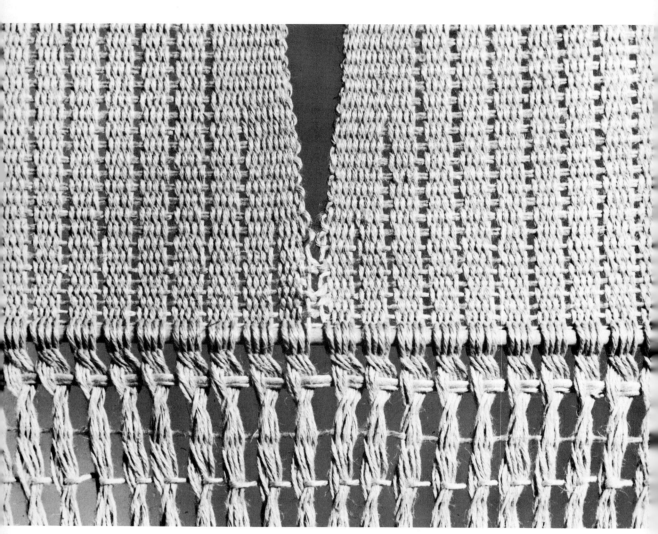

Fig. 128 THE BRIDE (detail), by Lenore Tawney, U.S.A., showing woven form. Plain weave and leno. *Photo by Ferdinand Boesch.*

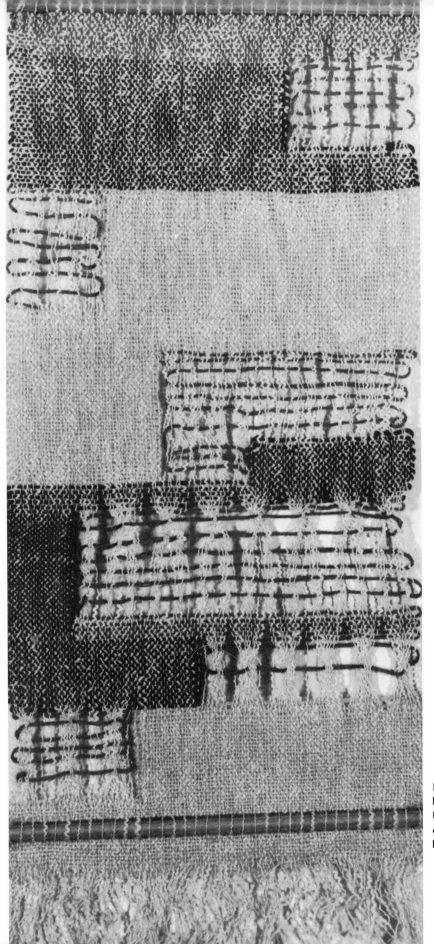

Fig. 129 Wall hanging by Lili Blumenau, U.S.A. Plain weave and fancy leno combined.

Fig. 130 Sampler, with six bands of techniques, made by student of Lili Blumenau's at Penland School of Crafts. *Photo by Harvey Chase.*

Some of the ideas inspired by this technique can be repeated in various proportions and yarns. Twist some warp threads for about 2 inches, then weave a band or width of plain weave. If this process is continued upward, you will get an enchanting pattern of open and closed bands. Or an equally enchanting frame can be made in plain weave with the inside in leno.

An infinite number of exceptionally beautiful textural effects can be created in double cloth, all apart from techniques that are highly specialized or involved. With a bottom layer in rib or plain weave the unwoven yarns from the top layer can be twisted in regular or irregular groups to produce an extremely arresting design. Or if you choose for each row of twisting a different group you will achieve most unusual effects. You may also divide the hanging into rectangles, and plan some in plain weave and others in double cloth with the twisting variety on top of plain weave. There are Peruvian and Mexican examples of this technique that are masterpieces of skilled craftsmanship, and are enhanced as well by the addition of striking color combinations. They more than repay careful study.

One may also use a combination called Greek leno. The leno here may consist of ten threads, and the design may be completed with Spanish lace weave. But if one prefers, the Spanish lace can be used all the way through. If this is done, space should be left between the warp threads for aesthetic balance and structural differentiation. Both old and present-day weavers also use Spanish lace on top of tapestry backgrounds (Fig. 131).

All the techniques described above are typical weaving constructions adaptable for tapestries and wall hangings. But twining, knotting, and macrame can be employed apart from these techniques and one does not need a loom to make them.

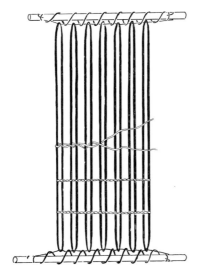

Fig. 132 Twining technique on a warp laced to a round stick on either side.

TWINING

To do simple twining, for instance, all one actually needs is an old picture frame or a painter's stretcher. This was perhaps the most ancient kind of interlacing (Fig. 132). It was used by our ancestors who needed carriers for

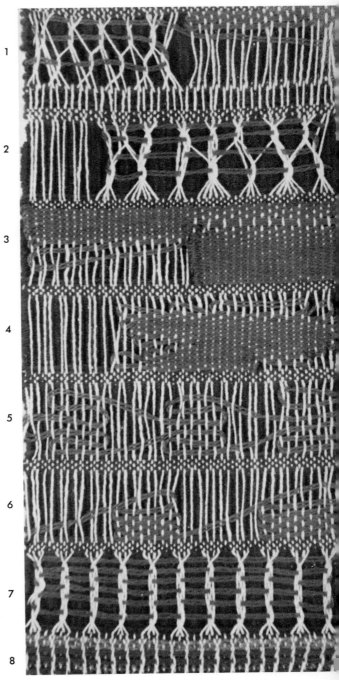

Fig. 131 Sampler with eight bands of techniques, by Lili Blumenau, U.S.A. (Top to bottom): 1. cloth and two-warp leno; 2. double cloth lower section in tapestry, upper in leno; 3 and 4, Spanish lace weave and tapestry underneath; 5 and 6, tapestry on rib weave; 7 and 8, fancy leno on tapestry background.

small children, food, and other household portables. They found that by bending and joining plaited and twined mats, they could make carriers that were, in effect, baskets. Among modern American weavers such a colorful improvisation is unknown, although its revival would offer interesting possibilities.

To make basic twining, string the warp around the frame rather tightly or use the method shown in the accompanying diagram (Fig. 132). For this warp use jute, or, for twining somewhat thinner material, cord that is not very heavy. For joining use a long double string, almost twice as long as the width of the material. Begin on the left selvage and lock the string into warp threads 1 and 2, then turn the double string, with one thread on top of the other. When the underneath thread passes under the next two warp yarns, continue all across the warp, as in the diagram.

You may twine in this same fashion diagonally, and make triangles of other shapes. This is usually done by first twining horizontally across the construction and then moving the desired figures by hand. In another twining technique, make first one row as described, and then turn the double string around pairs. For the next row split the warp pairs, starting with warps 2 and 3. This method can be varied individually and interpreted in contemporary style. But in all these twining procedures it is wise to make occasional attach-

ments to the frame upright of the loom to keep the hanging from narrowing in as the work progresses. (Maori weaving serves as an excellent example here.)

Various types of decoration may be introduced by passing another colored yarn around and under the twisted rows. You may also take long yarn strands, fringes, and odds and ends of left-over loom fabrics and tie them into the twined strings. If the warp is coarse and stiff, as it should be for twined weaving, and the tucks of the braid are drawn tight, you will find that this makes a highly satisfactory finish for a wall hanging.

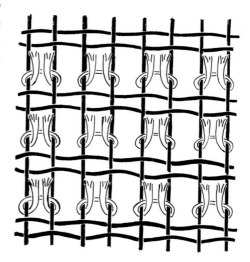

Fig. 133 Diagram represents two-weft plain weave alternating with one row of knots tied around two warp yarns. Knots made here with short ends of yarn are called Giordes knots.

KNOTTING

Rug techniques, like knotting and soumak, are also used for making wall hangings (Fig. 133). The various long and short knots are usually used in combination with other constructions. But a wall hanging can be composed entirely of intricately woven knots. In Norway, Sweden, and several other European countries rugs are frequently hung on the wall for decorative purposes. And this custom is not entirely unknown or ignored in America, although it is less common today than it was four or five generations ago.

Most weavers are familiar with the Giordes, or Turkish, knot. It is formed on two adjacent warp threads. A short piece of yarn—or, in practice, the end of a long piece from a ball, the piece being afterward cut off—is laid across and in front of the warp threads, and each of its ends is passed around one of them and emerges between them, as shown in the accompanying diagram. It is then pulled firmly downward toward the previous weaving. This is done either all across the construction, or—in a wall hanging —only where it is needed. A knot is tied on each pair of warp threads, and when the next and subsequent rows are thus secured, the same warp threads are kept paired. Two or four rows of plain weave are then commonly made between the knotted rows. The length of the knots is a matter of individual pref-

Fig. 134 Wall hanging or rug, by Tashiko Takaetzu, U.S.A. Technique in Giordes knots.

erence and the nature of the yarn—particularly its size—determines the overall texture of the rug or wall hanging. Some weavers prefer the Persian technique, and others the Scandinavian method.

The appearance of the knots in the Scandinavian method does not differ markedly from the way Persian knots look when they have been securely tied in patterns that are otherwise similar. In both instances the Giordes knot is used, and it is only the method that differs.

A gauge bar or long, wide stick is required for this type of weaving. It consists of a piece of metal that varies in width from ½ to ¾ of an inch, with a slit down one edge. The metal gauge is put across the material, and the yarn that is used for knotting unwinds from a small ball or from the inside of a yarn that is wound crosswise between the thumb and little finger. (Weavers call this a butterfly.) When the gauge bar is placed on the material, the yarn is guided around and underneath it to make the Giordes knot, as shown in the diagram (Fig. 133).

All these techniques give a great deal of texture to what would otherwise be an extremely flat surface. When they are applied wherever they are needed, they serve both a functional and an aesthetic purpose. For instance, thin surfaces go very well with long fringed loops and in tapestry-woven backgrounds short or long loops are often incorporated to heighten the beauty of a texture's weft-and-warp effects.

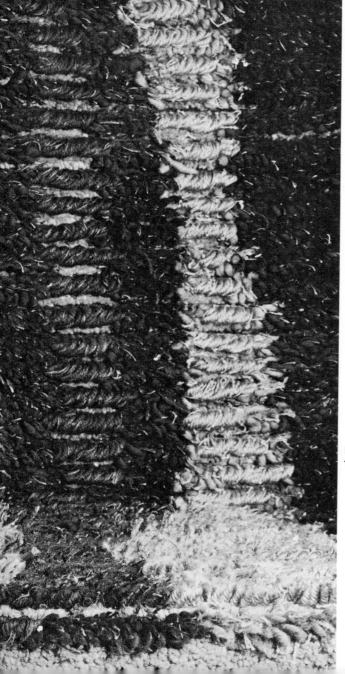

Fig. 135 Detail of wall hanging by Tashiko Takaetzu, U.S.A.

Opposite:
Fig. 136 INTERPLAY AFTER MORTON GOULD MUSIC, wall texture by Helen Kroll Kramer, U.S.A. Technique is in hooked loops on fabric background. *Photo by Eric Pollizer.*

Fig. 137 Wall hanging for an office in Mexico, by George Wells. Design is in hooked knots.

Fig. 138 Wall hanging by George Wells. Hooked-knots technique.

Fig. 139 Diagram represents macrame technique.

MACRAME

There is one technique, however, that absolutely cannot be worked out on a loom. In the ancient macrame technique the weaver takes a long piece of wooden board and puts in a row of nails. Then long pairs of yarns are tied around each of the nails and securely knotted. This forms the first row. The worker now ties another string around his waist to create the tension that is needed for macrame weaving. In this revived technique texture, color, and pattern can be brilliantly combined in many new, inventive interpretations. The artist-craftsman can also start weaving on the loom, and then knot the long hanging ends after the tapestry is cut from the loom (Fig. 139).

There is a constant interrelatedness between the techniques used in the weaver's craft and the material itself. In the techniques described in this chapter I have tried to make that very clear. There are many more techniques in which this interrelatedness plays just as vital a role, and some of these the weaver will discover for himself, for there is a limitless area of experimentation and innovation open to him. Here I have given the most important essentials, in the hope that they will guide and inspire him as his experience deepens and his technical skill becomes increasingly assured.

There is virtually no limit to the amount of experimenting that can be done in tapestry and wall-hanging techniques. Figured art weaving has been popular ever since man first adopted the idea of combining vertical and horizontal threads. The joy of selecting yarns and colors and combining them served the early weaver for purposes of independent expression as well as manufacture of apparel and household fabrics. Tapestry became the most versatile form of weaving —a traditional art expression with a store of technical procedures. Weavers and public alike welcome today's renaissance of this great textile art.

Weavers produce according to the needs of time, place, and artist. Peruvian, French, Scandinavian weavers—weavers of all nations— vary their output of yardage with tapestry production. The ideas, life, art, and religion that are expressed in clay, stone, paint, and metal may also be expressed in thread.

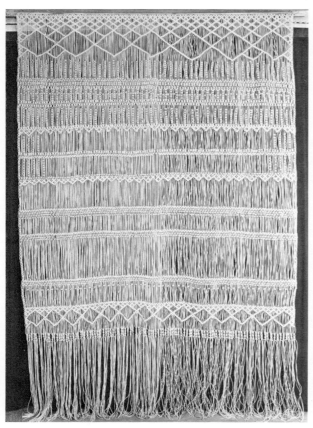

Fig. 140 Wall hanging in macrame and long fringes, by Spencer Depas. *Photo by Monika Reichelt.*

Fig. 141 Another wall hanging in macrame (detail), by Spencer Depas, Haiti. *Photo by Monika Reichelt.*

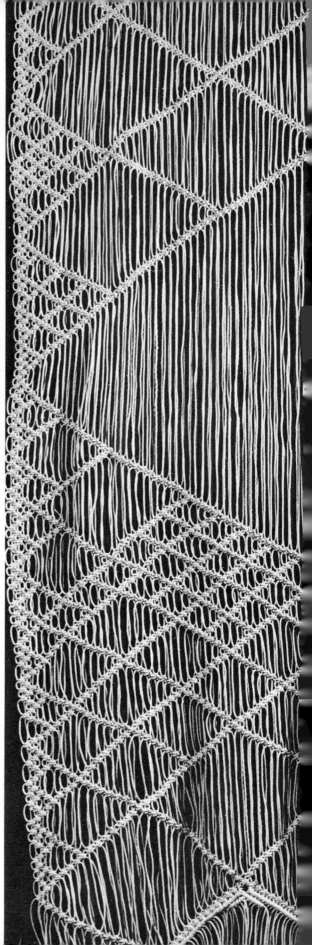

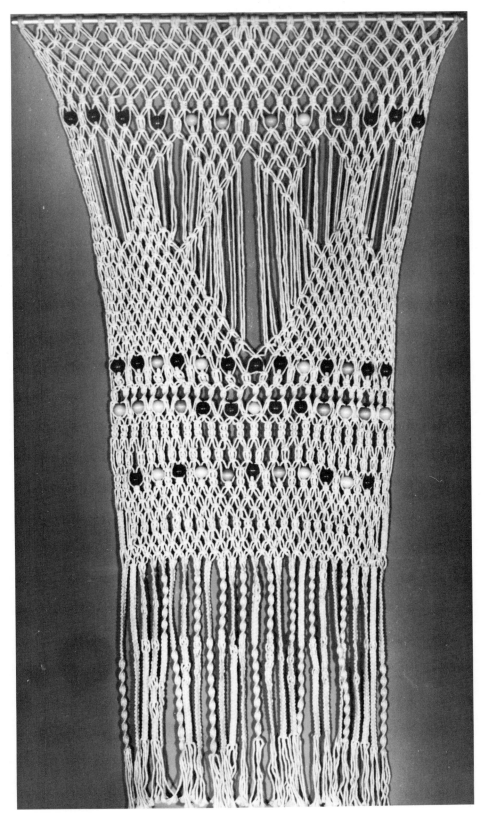

Fig. 142 Wall hanging, macrame and wooden beads, by Spencer Depas. *Photo by Monika Reichelt.*

Chapter 9

Making a Wall Hanging

WHEN YOU HAVE MAS-tered the techniques— your loom, the yarns, weaving procedures and weaves— there will no longer be any need to postpone creating a wall hanging of your choice. Owing to the technical nature of weaving, a designer must prepare his project before he makes a warp and sets up a loom. We have to know what we want to do—to keep the subject or idea clearly in mind.

We may make a composition of small and large geometrical shapes, squares, triangles, and diamonds.

Free forms and other abstractions are often favored, especially by beginners. You might look at a plant at home, then draw it precisely as you see it, and without elaboration. One does not have to be an accomplished sketch artist for this task, for afterward it will be done in yarns and weaves. Do not be disturbed by what you may feel to be deficiencies in the sketch itself—the subject will be reproduced with yarns and colors in a different medium. The sketch is merely designed to serve as a rough guide for a wall hanging.

Fig. 143 TROPICAL COUNTRY, by Lili Blumenau, U.S.A. Created from memory in various traditional and invented techniques.

STEP ONE—THE SUBJECT

There are many subjects from which to choose. Just look around you and dream a little. Do not think at this point about specific techniques. Regardless of where you live, you are surrounded by objects of decorative appeal, and if you live in the country there will be tree-shaded lawns or woodland vistas to widen your choice of subject matter. Sketch a few houses as you would like to have them look afterward on a tapestry. They can be large or small, isolated or in groups. Study paintings, particularly the work of such masters as Paul Klee. We can naturally learn a great deal from the tapestries woven in the past. The Peruvian and Coptic weavers derived much of their inspiration from objects in their immediate surroundings, and did truly beautiful work with animals and all kinds of leaves and flowers.

Contemporary weavers, whether city or country dwellers, will find that growing plants suggest an infinite variety of decorative designs, particularly if you give your imagination free rein. It is exciting to discover that this first important step in the creation of a tapestry that will be original and striking is a creatively stimulating undertaking.

Many people have the mistaken idea that the weaving of portraits is more difficult. But you will soon discover that if you approach the task without a set determination to make a completely realistic portrait of a specific figure you will succeed admirably. Study some of the illustrations in this volume for inspiration. The Egyptian portraits are not at all realistic, but they are fascinating in texture, and their brilliance of coloration more than compensates for their lack of realism.

Stories and legends—both popular and sacred—provide an abundance of inspiration in tapestry making. The lady and the unicorn is a secular story dating back to the Middle Ages, but it is still widely used by contemporary tapestry weavers. Today abstractions of people walking on the beach or through the woods amid patterns of light and shade are highly popular. Coptic weavers depicted Greek gods and many other mythological subjects. A favorite European subject was the representation of huntsmen, with bugles and falcons very much in evidence, and this theme has never been abandoned.

Sacred subjects are known all over the world and are used in all crafts. The cross has been depicted in many variations, and this sacred symbol will always figure prominently in weaving. In medieval times the events of the Bible were depicted extensively in both small and large tapestries, and this still holds true today.

Having decided on a subject we are now ready to proceed with the next step.

Fig. 144 RENAISSANCE,
by Eva Antilla, Finland.
Photo by Nousiainen.

STEP TWO—THE SKETCH

Whether you have chosen an abstract or realistic scene several experimental sketches should be made until you are satisfied that one of them is in close accord with the subject as you have visualized it. Shape distribution is of primary importance and after that the color scheme. In the shape distribution one tries to observe an overall balance. Color distribution depends largely on personal preferences, trends, and experience. The first small drawings do not need to be detailed.

Many weavers make a second enlarged drawing from the first small experimental ones. For this purpose you can use a piece of brown wrapping paper a little larger than the projected tapestry. In this way you have the subject before you in full scale. When one begins the weaving process, the full-size sketch is then placed under the warp, and fastened to it.

You will find this very convenient, because the outline is constantly in view, and more direct attention can be given to the weaving process. Outlining is usually done with a thick pencil, a brush, or a marker. Other small sketches, in watercolors or crayon, can be pinned to the wall to assist you when the weaving involves strict attention to some specific small detail not included in the drawing.

Fig. 145 THE TABLETS, by Helen Kroll Kramer, U.S.A. The three Hebrew
words represent the concept of the Ten Commandments—compassion,
beauty, mercy.

Fig. 146 PINES AND ROCKS, MAINE, by Kay Sekimachi, U.S.A. *Photo by Raymond Narimatsu.*

STEP THREE—THE YARNS AND OTHER MATERIALS

We must now consider, in a generalized way, the many types of yarns, the various sticks and plastics, and the traditional wools for tapestry making. A truly contemporary weaver of wall hangings is mostly concerned with the aesthetic value of what he hopes to achieve. He is free to vary the surface of textures regardless of technical rules.

He uses all kinds of yarns. Plain or straight threads give flat structures, and novelty yarns are used when irregularities are desired. We have today an unbelievably large variety of yarns at our disposal. Yarns of all types are made in the United States of America, and we can get interesting types from other parts of the world. There is no limitation on variety of weft yarns, but when we think about warp yarns we must keep technique—the tension factor—in mind. You can use curly and irregular yarns for the warp, but here experience and sometimes no small amount of courage are guiding factors.

The stiff materials have a great attraction for many weavers today, and some specialize in them. Some work with thin bamboo-like sticks or plastic rods. Others prefer to work with shapes cut from acetate sheets that are painted to suit a particular composition. Still another group of weavers has a strong preference for plant forms and dried flowers, and some find that shells, beads, and feathers provide more scope for highly individualistic expression.

The tapestry weaver working in

Fig. 147 MOTHER AND CHILD, by Martta Tiapole, Finland.

the traditional way is bound by yarn conventions. For instance, warp strength is determined by the warp set and the coarseness and fiber strength of these yarns. Here a specific, multiplied thread is needed. Since the warp is stretched tautly, the raw material must possess good tensile strength. But the warp yarns must also have a certain elasticity, because the sheds are made by stretching alternate warps into the triangular positions through which weft is placed, then going back to the flat stage and recovery from stretching. The warp threads must withstand above-average abrasion, since there will be more weft beating and manual manipulation in this procedure.

The rigors of these requirements are met by the use of cotton skein or cable twine, a several-ply, tightly twisted cord of smooth, long-staple, high-grade cotton. Size 6 is usually taken for an average set of ten to twelve ends per inch. If you prefer eight or nine ends per inch, use a heavier kind, and for a fine tapestry a fine type of yarn is naturally required.

Traditional tapestry weft is commonly thought of as wool. It was the fiber used during the great periods of European tapestry making. Silk has also been used for highlights and occasionally cotton. Quite often precious metal effects were achieved with real gold and silver threads. The French weavers now use a single type of yarn, also available in this country. It is a handsome, single-ply type of woolen yarn that gives a good coverage, and it is, as well, very strong and elastic.

STEP FOUR—COLOR

There is no aspect of a wall hanging's total composition that attracts the eye of the beholder more instantly than the color—or colors—the artist has used in creating it. Almost all the world's great painters have been perceptively aware of the importance of color, and have known how to make genius-inspired use of it.

Some people have so highly developed a color sense that the slightest disharmony grates on them and provokes at least a slight twinge of mental anguish. Others, more auditory-minded, are less disturbed when colors clash a little, and may even find the disharmony pleasing. But no matter what special aptitude

—or color-sense deficiency—the artist may discover in himself or how much other aspects of a wall hanging's composition may attract him, color remains an indispensable factor in the craft of weaving.

Colors may or may not have personalities of their own—the mystically inclined believe that they do —but there can be no doubt that the human mind has endowed them with a high degree of individuality. Red is quite different from green and purple from yellow, and we respond in different ways to colors that are warm and glowing and those that seem to us cold and dispiriting.

Seeing and feeling color—really

Fig. 148 LA VAGUE, by Mary Dambiermont. Tapestry.

seeing and feeling it and becoming intuitively aware of its nuances— is the best kind of preparation for a disciplined use of it. There are no theoretical outlines for the use of color, but we can gain valuable information by experiment, study, and practice. Even when one's color sense is not very highly developed, it is possible to go far beyond mere accidental employment of this element.

The source of all color is light, and without light there would be no visible configuration or texture in the objects that surround us and that we can become visually aware of only when our eyes, which are constructed to receive intricate re-

Fig. 149 AUTUMN, by Lili Blumenau, U.S.A.
Photo by Ferdinand Boesch.

Fig. 150 THE CROSS, by Mariane Strengel, U.S.A.

Fig. 151 ABSTRACTION, by Janice Bornt, U.S.A.

flections of light waves, transfer their message to the brain.

The unit of colored light man has adopted for his convenience in the systematic classification of light waves is called the solar, or prismatic, spectrum. The same prismatic pattern exists in nature, and the rainbow, with its six divisions of red, orange, yellow, green, blue, and violet, is perhaps the most commonly recurring and familiarly known example of just what a visible spectrum looks like when it is enlarged to sky-spanning dimensions.

There are many gradations of hues between each of the colors. Our perception of a hue is based on the particular wavelength of the light that produces it. The longer waves of light produce warm tones, the shorter, cool tones. But when light rays of all colors are combined we see only white, or achromatic light. Color perception depends on two visual sensations—chromatic (with hue) and achromatic (without hue).

The various colors of the spectrum—whether red, green, or blue—have different values and intensities. Color gradations range from light to dark. Value is the term used

Fig. 152 PAINTED DESERT, by Helen Kroll Kramer, U.S.A. *Photo by Oliver Baker Associates*

to indicate the amount of light a surface reflects. White is above or beyond the color range, or spectrum, and black is below it. All other color tones, chromatic and achromatic, fall between. When we speak of a color's purity we mean that neither black nor white nor any other neutral tone has been added to it. A pure red, for example, cannot be reduced to a neutral shade without weakening the color's intensity.

In wall hangings colors are usually used in combinations. The tone of a color—its dimension or value, hue, and intensity—changes with its use. There is a complete interrelationship between tones in a composition. The influence of one color on another depends not alone on their color qualities but also on the visual quantity each color occupies. A bright-green yarn, for instance, that looks subdued next to gray threads, will be luminous in total weft surface appearance. It is imperative for a weaver to study color theory and composition in both paintings and nature.

Colors can be put together to achieve either monochromatic or polychromatic contrast. A monochromatic contrast consists of two or more values, or intensities, of a single color—two shades of red, for instance, or a brilliant green with a neutral shade. When differing colors are combined, a polychromatic effect results—light blue with dark green, for example, or light red with orange and purple.

In proximity to black, most colors look brilliant, whereas when we place these same colors next to white they look subdued. In the realm of *hue* contrast, one encounters a wide variety of changes. The difference between hues is qualitative, whereas the value changes are quantitative.

"Temperature" change has a decided effect on hue contrasts. If an area of green is placed next to bright blue, the green will turn warm and yellowish. But the same green, with a warmer tone—a red or yellow—will appear cool and much less colorful.

When colors change, in their content or dimensions, they influence the area they occupy. When we place a light color next to a darker, in equal amounts, the light area will appear large and the dark area small. However, when we combine warm and cool colors, the warm divisions appear larger than the spaces made up of cool tones.

Psychological factors greatly influence color perception. We usually sense in reds, oranges, and yellows a warm and exciting atmosphere, and in blues and greens a kind of cool serenity. There are color combinations that remind us of Mexico or Guatemala.

Although most color experience remains on the level of sensation, the ability to discriminate between colors and appraise their value with insight and imagination is of the utmost importance in the making of wall hangings.

Fig. 153 VOODOO, by Mildred Fischer, U.S.A.

Fig. 154 PULPIT FALL, by Ted Hallman, U.S.A.

Fig. 155 HAPPY BIRTHDAY,
by Helen Kroll Kramer, U.S.A.

Fig. 156 HAITI, by Lili Blume-nau, U.S.A. *Photo by The Colony Studio of Boca Raton, Florida. Collection, Peter Moscher.*

STEP FIVE—WEAVING TECHNIQUES AND METHODS

We are now ready to take up the most vital aspect of the weaving procedure—the weave variations themselves. The plain weave, or up-and-down technique, is perhaps the most frequently used construction. It is easy to master and is the closest interlacing between warp and weft. One can go a long way by just acquiring a practical understanding of exactly what can be accomplished with the skillful use of plain weave.

Design expression is then achieved through a choice of yarns, color, and subject. With plain weave, for instance, one can make a wall hanging in different string proportions, using plain and novelty yarns, thick and thin types, in an all-red color scale. Each weave has its own character. To know and master all of them enlarges one's understanding of the entire weaving process, and is a worthy goal for the beginner to set for himself at the start. But the complete achievement of that goal is not necessary to create designs of striking originality and beauty.

If you want to understand weaves, you must first discover their visual forms and what they have to say. One of the most adventurous undertakings in wall-hanging composition is the search for weaves that correspond with the artists' original idea or vision.

A basic weave, such as the plain, does not in itself make an original wall hanging. That is achieved by interpretation and conversion of a basic construction. A painter, for instance, begins with a visualization of his idea of a particular flower or person which he wishes to embody on canvas. His flowers—if they are tulips—are only tulips, just as plain weave is only plain weave, an impersonal or general pattern.

In the finished painting, however, the tulips will be highly individualized, a new, often symbolic, form of the flower as it appears to his inner vision.

Just as the painter must first acquaint himself with the precise form of flowers in their natural state, so the weaver must learn all he can about visual impressions in fundamental weave constructions.

The artist-weaver will see the plain weave, for instance, as an overall structure, if the warp and weft are identical in yarn composition. He will notice that the yarn presents an even appearance, be-

cause the amount of yarn distributed in both directions, warp and weft, is equal. But when he uses a very thick weft yarn or acetate rod, the appearance of the plain weave will change. The crossings or stitches formed by the individual warp yarns become longer and more pronounced, and some very hard-to-use materials stay in their place and do not move.

If you use the plastic shapes of dried flowers on long stems, this kind of plain weave provides the best and safest solution. You may, for example, decide to make a transparent wall hanging in either plain weave or leno or some other twisted technique. An idea would be to use an irregular warp yarn—ratiné, widely spaced—and the weft from wool in plain weave loosely beaten. Because of its construction the irregular warp yarn will hold the loosely beaten wool weft, since plain weave interlaces closely all the threads.

In formal tapestry weaving, you have to work according to conventions. Weaving weft threads back and forth in two alternating sheds is a simple process, quickly mastered. But a tapestry is composed of many independent color areas, and joining them, forming the margins between them, requires special techniques.

Areas are developed in all forms with margins that follow horizontal, vertical, and diagonal lines, as well as various shadings and blendings of color.

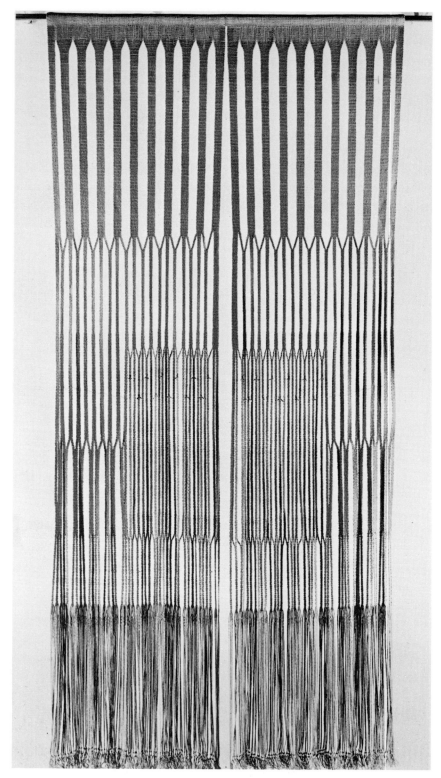

Fig. 157 ARK VEIL, by Lenore Tawney. *Photo by Ferdinand Boesch.*

183

Fig. 158 ARK VEIL (detail, gold wire around tassels), by Lenore Tawney. *Photo by Ferdinand Boesch.*

Fig. 159 ARK VEIL (detail, the fringes), by Lenore Tawney. *Photo by Ferdinand Boesch.*

EXAMPLE I

1. Subject
2. Sketch
3. Yarns
4. Color
5. Weaving technique
6. Loom set up
7. Weaving
8. Finishing the wall hanging

Subject

This project is an easy-to-make wall hanging. The subject, or motif, is a geometrical design. I decided on a combination of rectangles and horizontal bands. The next step was to make many sketches, all in different proportions. No thought was given to color or yarn. The emphasis was on good proportion and all-over balance (Fig. 160).

Sketch

The sketch that is selected may result from a spontaneous choice of the moment, based on immediate appeal. Here the choice was to make a small wall hanging measuring about 12 by 28 inches. It is always wise to choose uneven proportions because they are more rhythmic, and convey a more pronounced impression of movement. Take a large piece of brown wrapping paper and make an exact full-scale drawing. One can use a black marking pen or brush. Now one thinks about the values in black and white. This involves making visual

notations of the light-to-dark scale. Some rectangles will be more pronounced than others, and these will be indicated in black. A somewhat lighter group will be indicated in dark gray. Two of the groups should be very light, and for this expression two rectangles are sketched in a very light shade of gray, and some others represented by transparent threads. To show transparent areas on paper you imitate this structure with paint or a marker. Naturally, one can also write out the various values by making a penciled notation in each rectangle.

The Yarns

When such a full-scale sketch in black and white is completed, you have something concrete in front of you, and your mind begins to develop further ideas. Since several rectangles should be transparent, you decide to show the warp, and have no weft in these areas. Therefore the warp yarn must be interesting and definitely not a straight yarn, but a novelty bouclé style (Fig. 161).

The wefts will be in wool No. 6, two ply, which is rather thick. This yarn number gives only the size or quality, not the colors. The next step is to consult a color chart and find out what shades are available. We need two dark and very pronounced colors. These were the

Fig. 160 GEOMETRICAL
DESIGN, by Lili Blumenau,
U.S.A.

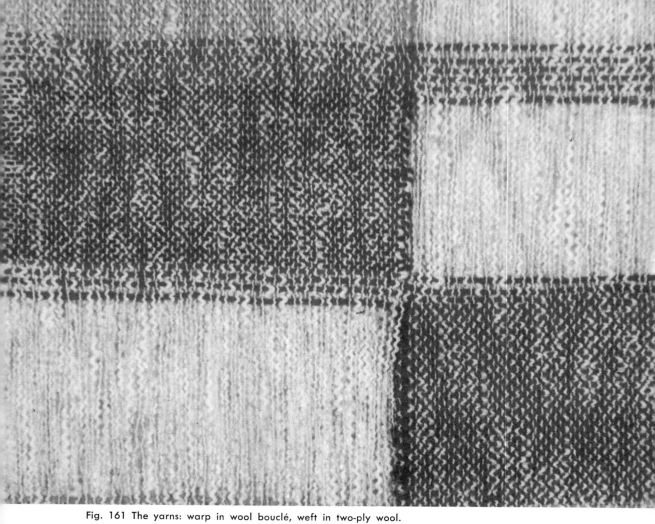

Fig. 161 The yarns: warp in wool bouclé, weft in two-ply wool.

Fig. 162 The weave: plain weave and unwoven warp.

black areas on the sketch. In the wall hanging they will be woven in dark-green wool. The intermediate or dark grays will be red, but somewhat more subdued than the bright green. Now we have to decide what color to choose for the light yarns. Yellow will look best, together with the green and red. The remaining light transparent rectangles do not require a decision, since no weft will be necessary. The warp alone will form a light transparent expression. If one wishes, one can now fill in colors on the full-size sketch. For some weavers this will prove helpful, but it is not essential.

So far, we have the visual plan —the overall design. Now the technical aspects of the weaving process become our major concern.

The Weave

The weave will be the simple plain-weave construction, and only the spacing of the warp yarns remains to be determined. We take 12 warp ends over 1 inch in length and multiply 12 by the width, in this case 12 inches. We shall need a total of 144 warp ends for this hanging. It should be about 28 inches long. To this 28 inches we will have to add at least 2 yards of additional length. This will be needed for the tying of the warp yarns at the warp and cloth beam by means of knots and bows. We need also additional length for the unwoven part of the warp that lies between the warp bunches and the beginning of the

tapestry, as well as for the part in back of the harnesses. One must also, of course, keep in mind the yarn's shrinkage. The warp is taut on the loom, and since it is of wool there will be more shrinkage than takes place in cotton yarns.

But it is wise in weaving to make allowances for more shrinkage than a too strict estimate would suggest, a rule that is commonly adhered to by all experienced weavers.

Winding the Warp

We now are prepared for the next step—winding the warp. Measure off a length of string 3 yards long. This includes 28 inches for the finished tapestry, plus allowances for loom waste and shrinkage at either hem or fringes. Tie this 3-yard guide string to the top cross peg and the end around the bottom outer peg of the reel. Take two spools with your warp yarn and place them on a spool rack. The weaver now stands with the warping reel at his left, the spool rack at the right, and ties the two yarn ends from the spools to the first peg on the upper crossbar of the reel (Fig. 163). With the right hand he separates and arranges the threads over and under the pegs to form a warping cross, in order to keep these threads in a consecutive alignment. The cross is formed between pegs 3 and 4, alternating one thread at a time, over and under, between the two pegs.

The weaver then revolves the reel and guides the threads around toward the right until the second crossbar and its two bottom pegs are reached. The distance between the top and bottom pegs is the warp length—3 yards. Two threads are now on the reel, each 3 yards long. From the bottom pegs—where the yarns are guided together, over and under—the weaver carries these yarns back up to the starting point while turning the reel in reverse. This back-and-forth turning of the threads between the start and finish pegs is continued until the necessary 144 lengths of warp yarn is measured out.

When all the necessary warp is on the reel, the crossing yarns are secured between the pegs on top and bottom crossbars with a long

Fig. 163 Winding the warp. *Photo by Len Depas.*

piece of yarn of different color from that of the warp.

Begin with the top cross, and put this tying yarn between the layers of pegs 3 and 4 (Fig. 164). Then draw it through these divisions, finally knotting the ends of the threads. The bottom cross is secured in the same way. When both crosses have been tied the warp, is ready to be taken from the reel.

Remove the warp from the top downward, wind around the wrist to form the first loop, and chain off, as in hand crocheting (Fig. 165).

Dressing the Loom

Now comes the loom setup, or dressing the loom. I employ here a procedure that is commonly used for short warps. Take two long

Fig. 164 Securing the warp cross between pegs 3 and 4. *Photo by Len Depas.*

strings, a little longer than the depth of the loom, and fasten these securely around the breast and back beams, after they have been guided through the heddle harnesses near the end of the loom. With another pair of strings repeat this procedure on the opposite side. Now, wind the warp around the back beam two or three times, and make sure that the top cross hangs down over the beam. Take two long, flat lease sticks and put one of them through one division of the yarn, and repeat this insertion with the other stick (Fig. 166).

The leash sticks are then secured into the two long strings fastened on either side of the loom. Tie the sticks together and remove the security thread that was tied on the warping reel. Draw the warp

Fig. 165 Removing the warp form the reel, making a chain, like hand crocheting. *Photo by Len Depas.*

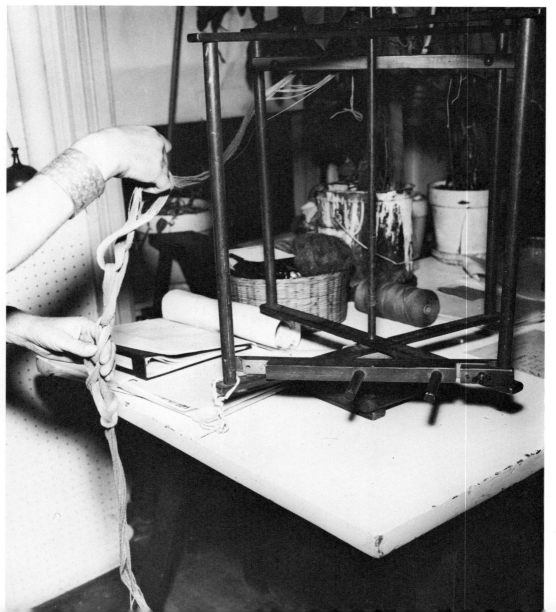

Fig. 166 One lease stick is put through a warp division of the cross formed on the warping reel.
Photo by Len Depas.

forward, toward the heddle eyes, and straighten out the yarns. When they have all been leveled and arranged in groups, you are ready for heddle threading (Fig. 167).

One after another the threads are drawn through the heddle eyes with an entering hook—a long, flat crocheting needle (Fig. 168). Draw the first warp end by putting the hook through the first heddle eye on the first shaft. Then take the second yarn and thread it through the first heddle on the second shaft. Put the third thread through the first heddle eye on the third shaft,

and the next yarn on the last, or fourth, frame—first heddle eye. This completes a threading unit of a straight regular draw threaded from front to back. Repeat this threading order until all of the yarns—in this case 144 ends—are carried through the heddle eyes. After twenty or thirty yarns have been threaded, tie them for security.

When the threading process is completed, all warp yarns should be put through the dents in the reeds. In this project of 12-ends-per-inch density, use a 12-dent-per-

Fig. 167 Warp yarns are ready for heddle threading. *Photo by Len Depas.*

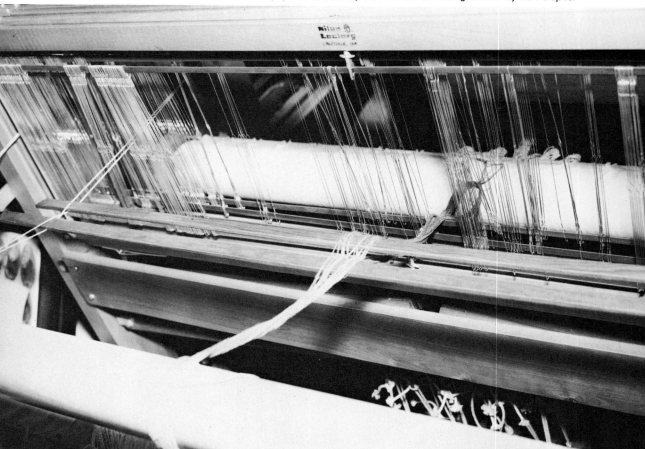

inch reed. One yarn is put through each dent, or opening. Before taking yarns through the dents, pull the warp toward the front so that the threads are long enough for easy handling. Begin reentering, also called "sleying," with the first thread, somewhat as in heddle threading. Put the hook through the dent, grasp the first yarn from shaft 1, and pull it through the dent. Repeat, hooking the next one through the next dent. Continue until all the yarns are dented. When finished, group-tie the threads so that they hang from the reed securely.

Sleying can be done either with the reed in the beater or removed from the beater and placed in a flat horizontal position, resting on the outside yarns for the lease sticks.

The group-tied warp threads, hanging in bunches from the reed in front of the loom, have now to be secured to the rod that is connected to the cloth roller. Before the warp tying is done, the extension cords, or apron, should be guided around the roller and over the breastbeam. Take a small bunch on the left-hand side, divide it into two parts,

Fig. 168 Heddle threading: one thread after another is drawn through a heddle eye. *Photo by Len Depas.*

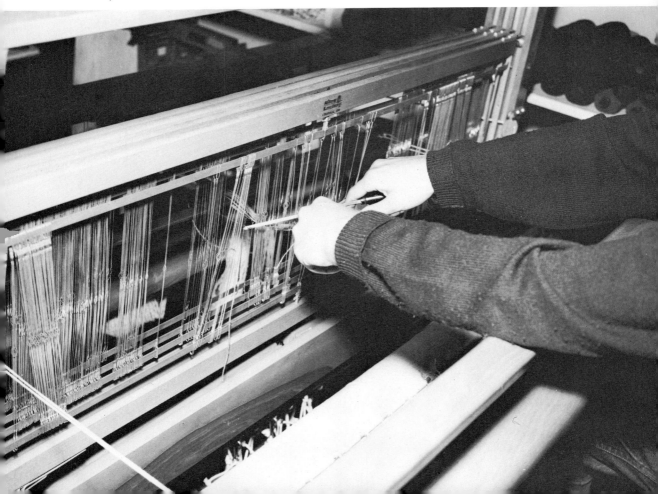

and put them over and around the rod, fastening them with a knot and half-bow (Fig. 169). Now tie the bunch on the opposite end and then the center group. The remaining groups should then be knotted in the same fashion to the rod. The yarns should be straightened before they are tied to the rod, so that they will remain level.

In this loom setup procedure, you next wind the warp around the front, or cloth, beam. Go in back of the loom and straighten out the warp, going through the yarns with your hand as if you were combing them. Also hold the whole warp fairly tight, and shake it. When the yarns are smooth and evenly leveled, wind them onto the front beam.

Into this short warp put a sheet of brown wrapping paper, for the yarns, being of ratiné wool, are uneven. When the warp is wound and the yarns hang behind the harnesses in back of the loom, you are ready for another group-tying.

First cut along the complete warp so that the yarns are of even length. Then group-tie as you did in front, around the rod. Be careful to do it in the center, a little wider than your project of 12-inch width. Warp winding is usually done by two persons, but on small looms it can be successfully accomplished by the weaver alone. If you have no assistance, hold the warp tightly and stand in front of the loom, approximately a foot away. Leaning

Fig. 169 Securing the warp to the loom in groups around a rod connected to the cloth beam. Photo by Len Depas.

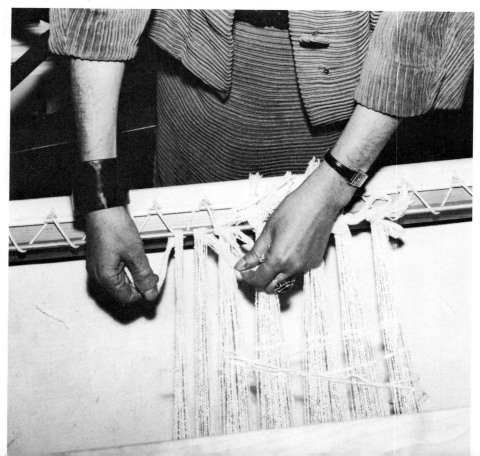

slightly forward will enable you to turn the back roller with ease. After some warp is on the roller, insert sheets of paper between the layers to prevent the soft yarns from forming grooves or uneven tensions. For this short warp, use about one sheet of brown wrapping paper, 18 inches by 2 yards in size. Winding is continued until the yarns in front hang down long enough for final group-tying around the rod, of cloth, beam.

When bunches are tied in the usual fashion, the yarns must be tightened by means of a ratchet wheel, on the right side of the cloth beam. Then you must test for evenness and tension by going over the warp surface with your hand. When this has been done, the shafts can be arranged for pattern or weave. In this project we take plain weave, and shafts 1 and 3 have to be raised alternately with shafts 2 and 4 together.

Weaving

Before beginning your weaving, you must prepare your shuttles. Fill them with four carefully chosen colored yarns. To have a good interlaced base, take any type of heavy yarn and weave about two inches before starting the project. Then take the shuttle with bright-green wool and weave all across the width for 2 inches. Secure the end and weave into the following shed. Have available a flat bamboo stick 2 inches wide that has been painted dark green. Raise half of the warp and insert the stick, which will provide both needed weight and serve as a decoration for the wall hanging's bottom (Fig. 170). Turn now

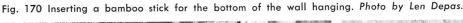

Fig. 170 Inserting a bamboo stick for the bottom of the wall hanging. *Photo by Len Depas.*

Fig. 171 Open the shed and enter weft yarn on the shuttle. *Photo by Len Depas.*

Fig. 172 Bringing the beater forward to press weft into warp. *Photo by Len Depas.*

Fig. 173 Turning around warp thread with shuttle, to weave the 7" x 2" rectangle. *Photo by Len Depas.*

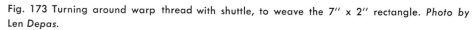

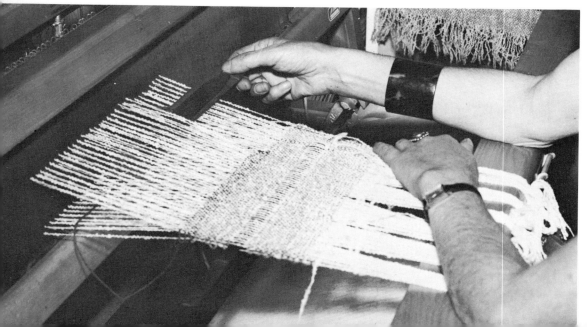

to the alternating shed and continue to weave with bright green for one inch (Figs. 171, 172).

Take the shuttle with magenta red wool and weave from the left side for 7 inches, then turn around the nearest warp yarn and return through the following shed (Fig. 173). Do this for 2 inches, turning around the warp thread loosely to get a straight vertical line. Take another flat shuttle with bright red, and weave all across five wefts and secure the thread end firmly. Now start from the right with the fourth shuttle having light-yellow wool, weave for 7 inches, turn around warp and return for the next shed, just as you did with the magenta yarn. Weave for 3 inches upward and secure the end. Make four wefts in magenta, again plain weave. With the bright red continue to weave a rectangle in the middle. Open warp to get through the shed with the shuttle, about 3 inches from the left edge. Weave 6 inches, turn around warp, and return in the following shed. Weave this part back and forth for 3 inches.

When the center 6-inch rectangle is finished, weave eight wefts with yellow wool across the whole width. Weave on the right side a 4½ by 3½ rectangle in magenta. Afterward make four wefts in bright red all across and another rectangle in bright green, 7¼ inches woven from left to right and 3 inches high. Now weave five wefts with the magenta wool and above it a light-yellow rectangle 7¼ inches

long from the left side and 2 inches high. Make five wefts in bright red over the whole width, the last one with the magenta. Start from the right side, weave a length 9 inches, and return. Continue for 3 inches and finish the wall hanging by weaving about 1 inch all across with this yarn.

Lay into a shed another flat bamboo stick—it will later be used for a yarn hanger—and after the stick has been introduced into the warp, weave with wool about 2

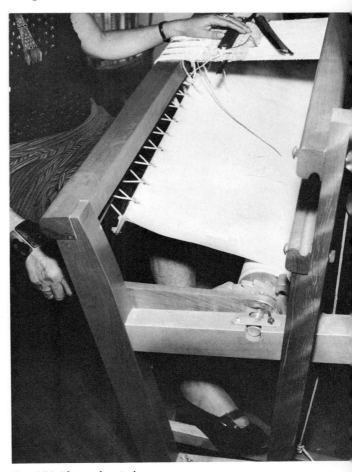

Fig. 174 After a few inches are woven, more warp length is needed. The weaver releases the warp beam by means of pressing a brake (lower right) with the foot. *Photo by Len Depas.*

inches to make a hem. The finished tapestry should be cut across its total width. First loosen the warp, then cut and put the hanging on a table for inspection and sewing. Sometimes small defects in weaving can be corrected and visible knots joined to the fabric by mending.

When you are satisfied that the tapestry is as perfect as it can be made, add a hem at the top—your first weft at the beginning below will hold firmly in the ratiné warp —and leave fringes about 2½ inches long. The tapestry is now ready for hanging.

EXAMPLE II

The study of designing presents a dilemma. Visual relations can be generalized, but structural relations must always be very detailed and specific. We are compelled to choose between studying actual examples of designing, in which the organic connection between visual and structural relationships is clear, or of concentrating on the general nature of these relationships.

In an analysis and discussion of visual relationships, we deal in a general way with the whole problem of designing, but sacrifice breadth of application. In structural analysis we risk a false emphasis on formal problems.

I have chosen to combine, to some extent at least, both methods in considering the design I have selected to illustrate the functional and aesthetic aspects of tapestry weaving, as they bear upon the various factors we have examined in theory. I will relate them to the causal factors of purpose, materials, and technique, so that we may have as broad a grasp as one example can give of the organic unity of design in action.

The first consideration that must be borne in mind before we undertake a composition problem analysis is the relation it bears to tapestry weaving in general. A problem can be so unusual and specialized that it sheds little light on the technical and aesthetic aspects of problems much wider in scope and of considerably more importance.

In the tapestry I have chosen, the technique is in general accord with procedures that are basic to the weaver's craft and the mastery of which is essential even for the beginner.

Every composition for a wall

hanging has two aspects, and we must not slight the one at the expense of the other. We must first of all consider the organization and expression of the ideas it is to contain. Organizational planning is of the utmost importance, and we must devote a great deal of thought to it. It should never be hurried. When we are completely satisfied with it —and not before—we can consider the physical form in which our ideas are to be presented. The first problem is one of content, imaginatively projected; the second concerns the actual tapestry spread out on the loom. The causal factors of purpose, form, material, and technique apply to both. This is true of all tapestries, but we can never completely grasp these problems abstractly. We must have, directly before us, an example that is concretely meaningful and can be analyzed in step-by-step fashion.

The example presented here was woven during a summer spent in the country. Its purpose can perhaps best be defined by considering how the idea for it grew. Country vistas have always enchanted me: woodland isles with autumn leaves descending or bright with early spring flowers, a garden viewed from a balcony, a mountain lake in the early spring. The eyes of a designer seldom remain blind to the many unusual aspects of nature that can be utilized artistically, and on that particular summer day it was the garden view from a balcony that entranced me the most.

I thought that someday I could make effective use of the visual patterns this view suggested, and made a rough sketch, indicating how the light and dark areas could be made to blend or combine in a contrasting way to enhance the beauty of a wall hanging. For a few weeks I forgot about that particular sketch, but the general motif remained alive in my mind. One morning, while I was working on a warp leftover on the loom, the particular color combination of yellows, greens, and blues reminded me of the garden view I had found so enchanting.

I went in search of the sketch, found it, and looked it over carefully. Although I was in my studio at the time, I seemed to be standing again on the balcony, staring out over the garden (Fig. 175). I saw again the wind-stirred branches, the somber tree trunks that cast long shadows, the bright and beautiful flowers.

I lost no time in gathering yarns, heavy threads, bouclés, some shiny, some dull, and a few decorative odds and ends. Ready at hand I now had all of the material I felt I would need—wool, rayon, linen, and cotton. All the yarns were in the shades I wanted for a composition of blues, greens, yellows, and a few neutrals. They were all a mixture of lights and darks, some in intermediate values. For the foreground, or ironwork balcony structure, I knew I would need some dark values in another color, and decided on a deep purple and just a touch of black.

Fig. 175 GARDEN VIEW, by Lili Blumenau, U.S.A. Combination of traditional and invented techniques. *Photo by Ferdinand Boesch.*

Since the warp consisted of many different raw materials, arranged in irregular stripes, I decided also that it would be a mistake to cover up these values. I knew that I would have to improvise a bit, and use several different weave methods. I was fascinated by the thought that I could show the warp at intervals, if I so desired, and with the true tapestry method hide it whenever the evolving design made its concealment essential.

In my mind's eye I began to have a clear picture of the many weaves I intended to employ, and as they passed in review before me I had no difficulty in visualizing what the finished wall hanging would be like in size and form content.

When organization of the idea content had been worked over in other sketches, I studied some of my former work for weave possibilities.

Sometimes the term "functional" is used to describe this kind of preliminary tapestry planning, but if it is employed in a strictly utilitarian sense it is very wide of the mark here. I am always working toward a satisfying visual composition in which the tone and texture of the weave, the subject, and other elements are effectively related. Utilitarian considerations, when they exist at all, are subordinated to the aesthetic value of the pattern as it evolves, and in the search for the right weave or weaves to carry out an idea, no nonaesthetic considerations are allowed to intrude. I have always worked this way, and hope that I always shall, regardless of the end purpose a tapestry may have been designed to serve. Whether weaving is pursued for pleasure or profit, beauty of design—as well as a constant striving for excellence in the selection of materials that will contribute to a wall hanging's harmony and balance—should be the artist's primary concern.

When, as sometimes occurs, functional considerations suggest certain weaves, and they fit in with established traditions, and approximate weaves used in medieval and other early textiles, as well as in many contemporary designs, their inclusion does no violence to the artistic integrity of the work as a whole. Familiarity with tradition automatically enters the designing process by influencing our judgments as we work out the balance of factors with which we have to deal. This is just another way of saying that because of well-established and deeply ingrained working habits, unconscious as well as conscious, impulses influence our choice of materials and decorative motifs, and we are never completely free—nor is it desirable—to run the loom in any way that may momentarily strike our fancy. It may be true to say that we can go through the motions. But if we do so in defiance of all aesthetic impulses, unconscious or otherwise, the finished work will be a caricature of what we set out to accomplish.

With the original balcony-garden vista and the sketches inspired by it, as well as the form-content organizational plan kept firmly in mind, I wind some yarn on a shuttle and begin to weave. I work at first in plain weave with a good straight yarn, taking care to keep my width —from 2 to 6 inches—even as I proceed. Also, I put into the first warp two long lease sticks, and after I have woven a few inches of plain weave I insert under the warp brown paper corresponding in size to the form-content projection of the finished wall hanging. On this paper I draw an outline in dark ink of a few preliminary patterns to assist me as I go along. No actual weaves or colors are marked at this point.

I know how the lower part should look, and can proceed without risking too great a departure from even minor aspects of the overall organizational plan. I cannot, of course, go back and appraise the exact extent of my success in that respect, and intuition and experience are my sole guides here.

Experience and intuition do not embrace all the essential qualities a weaver must bring to his or her art. But in the preliminary stages of tapestry creating they play a major role, and this is particularly true of intuition. To begin a tapestry with nothing but cold logic as a guide would be to risk early and quick disaster, for the creative weaver has only a limited ability consciously to analyze the importance of every first-step procedure. Here feeling must be his guide, for every yarn

surface has a characteristic texture, and the effect it will have on other yarn surfaces must be instinctively sensed.

He cannot afford too many mistakes, even minor ones, in creating the preliminary patterns in an organizational design. The entire process is in a sense experimental, but certain definite motifs and their variations must be established at the start; and if too great a departure from the original plan occurs here, further improvisation, no matter how brilliant, may fail to repair the harm that has been done to the overall weave construction.

The great medieval weavers were aware of this pitfall, and we have only to study the traditional masterworks they produced to realize how important a part intuition must have played at the very beginning of the weaving process.

It is true that I do a great deal of revising while working at the loom, and not infrequently totally new organizations arise. But if one starts with a vitally stimulating and unusual idea in mind, it can be painfully—almost tormentingly— frustrating to have to go back and rework it and perhaps lose one's original inspiration entirely. A work that is attempted for the second time is seldom as boldly original in design as it might have been if one had carried the original plan to a successful conclusion.

We must not let this happen with the enchanting garden view from a balcony that we have chosen

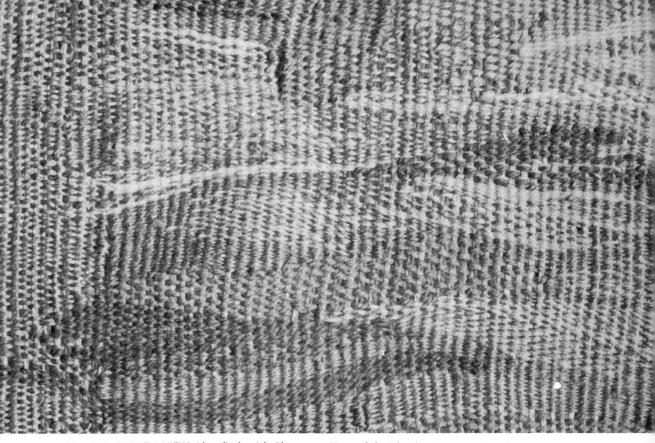

Fig. 176 GARDEN VIEW (detail), by Lili Blumenau. Upper left side showing curved wefts.

Fig. 177 GARDEN VIEW (detail), by Lili Blumenau. Lower right part showing open and close weave.

as an example here. So let us return to the loom and consider the color variations that must now be woven into the tapestry. As a general rule, not all the darkness should be in one place. But how confusing and frequently unnecessary such a rule-of-thumb restriction can be, particularly when there is a cluster of darkly looming trees in the background that can set off the bright clusters of flowers in the middle foreground with telling effect. In this case we shall ignore the rule, and work in the darker colors with discrimination and restraint precisely where they should appear in the finished tapestry.

Finally the weaving is completed. Every possibility of creating novel and exciting color combinations, unusual contrasts, and strikingly original warp-and-weft effects has been explored and taken full advantage of. There has been no slighting of experimentation except in those instances where a rigid procedure must be followed to maintain the integrity of the design as a whole.

We are now ready for the next step, the actual removal of the tapestry from the warp. First, we examine all the hanging threads. Since the tapestry will hang on the wall with the reverse side concealed, cutting them, we decide, would make no sense, since none of them are sufficiently long to dangle visibly. At the bottom of the piece we now lay a long curtain rod or wooden stick, and repeat the same procedure on the top. Hemstitching of the plain woven fabric material in proximity to the rods holds them securely in place.

The actual hanging of a wall tapestry can be something of an event. Like all artists, the weaver is not likely to take pride in his work if it does not receive some measure of recognition and praise. Even when dissatisfied with what he has accomplished, he would not be human if harsh criticism did not disturb him and a complete lack of praise seem to him, at times, even more deadly. So it is almost with fear and trembling that he brushes all misgivings aside, hangs his newest creation on the wall, and invites his friends in to look at it.

Sometimes he is delightfully surprised, and sometimes bitterly disappointed. But as a rule, if the wall hanging gives him pleasure—if he feels that he has tried very hard and has succeeded in what he set out to accomplish—praise will overwhelmingly predominate.

Glossary of Terms

Beater The frame that holds the reed and that is used to beat the weft.

Bobbin The spool, the quill, or the tube on which the weft thread is wound.

Breastbeam The front beam over which the cloth passes on its way to the cloth beam.

Cloth beam The roll in the front of the loom on which the finished cloth is wound.

Cross The crossing in the threads of either or both ends of the warp. This cross holds the warp threads in place, and prevents tangling.

Dent The space between the vertical bars of the reed through which the warp threads are strung or guided.

Dressing the loom This is the complete process of preparing the loom for weaving.

Fiber Substance made up of threadlike parts, limited in length, that are twisted together for fabric making.

Filling Another name for weft yarns.

Harness The frame or shaft on which the heddles are hung. Looms have several frames or shafts.

Heddle eye The opening in the middle of the heddle.

Heddles The string, wires, or flat steel that is hung from dowels or harness to hold the warp threads in place, in making a shed.

Lam Any of the lower levers connected by cords between harnesses and treadles in various looms to enable the weaver to bring down the harness with one foot.

Lease The same as the warping cross.

Loom The tool or machine that is the cloth-weaving instrument. It ranges from the simplest wooden frame to the most intricate power-driven apparatus of modern industry.

Plain weave   The interlacing of warp and weft in the closest weaving method. It resembles mending.

Ply   Denotes the number of strands wound together to form the yarn.

Ratchet   A wheel with a tooth edge fastened to the end either of a cloth beam or of a warp beam to control the winding action.

Reed   The part of the beater that holds the threads an equal distance apart, and determines the firmness of the cloth. It also helps to beat the weft into place.

Reed hook   A hook to draw the warp threads through the dents in the reed.

Shed   The opening of the warp threads between which the shuttle containing the weft thread is passed.

Shuttle   A small flat stick or boat that holds the weft yarn for weaving.

Skein   A hank or a loosely coiled length of yarn.

Spool rack   A rack or frame that holds spools of yarn.

Tabby   The same as plain weave; another name for the mending-type weave.

Tension   The stretch of the warp threads during the process of weaving.

Threading   The guiding or drawing of warp threads through the heddle eyes.

Treadles   The pedals at the bottom of the loom, operated by foot, that raise or lower the harnesses to make a shed.

Twist   The turning of the thread.

Warp   The threads running lengthwise in the loom.

Warp beam   The beam at the back of the loom on which the warp is wound.

Warping   The process of putting the warp onto the warp beam of the loom.

Warping reel or mill   A revolving frame on which large warps are made and guided from top to bottom.

Weft   The threads interwoven horizontally with the warp to make a fabric.

Index